Ret
to
South Africa

Chris Wilson

Disclaimer

This publication is designed to provide accurate and authoritative information in regard to emigrating and retiring to South Africa. However, it is sold with the understanding that the author and publisher are not engaged in rendering immigration, legal, accounting or other professional services.

One of our observations throughout this entire process is that although the 'rules' don't change, their interpretation does. Therefore, if in doubt you should consult an appropriate competent professional person.

This book contains a number of references to third parties that were used. In the majority of cases, they provided excellent service and are therefore recommended.

All trademarks, brands and companies referred to in this book are for illustrative purposes only. They are the property of their respective owners and not affiliated with this publication in any way.

Copyright © 2017 Chris Wilson

All rights reserved.

ISBN: 9781973336648

Contents

Disclaimer i
Preface viii
Acknowledgments... ix
Part 1 - Why South Africa.................................... 1
   1. Why South Africa?...................................... 2
      1.1 Climate 2
      1.2 Language 5
      1.3 Permanent Right to Reside 6
      1.4 Income Tax-Friendly............................ 7
      1.5 Extensive Expatriate Community 8
      1.6 Medical Facilities............................... 11
      1.7 Domestic Help 11
   2. Why Not? 12
      2.1 Corruption 12
      2.2 Crime 13
      2.3 Frozen UK State Pension 15
Part 2 – Before Departure................................. 16
   3. Visas 17
      3.1 Retired Person's Visa......................... 17
      3.2 Financial Independent Permit 27(F).... 25
      3.3 Retired Person's Permanent Permit 27(E) 26

3.4 Should I Apply for a Visa or Permit?...................27
4. Health Care..29
   4.1 Private Medical Insurance...................................29
   4.2 Hospital Cash Plans 30
   4.3 Medical Aid...30
   4.4 Healthcare Costs and Inflation 36
   4.5 Pre-Existing Medical Conditions..........................36
5. Telecommunications 37
   5.1 Land Lines..37
   5.2 Mobile Phones 40
6. Banking..41
   6.1 UK Banking 41
   6.2 South African Banking 42
7. Foreign Exchange 46
   7.1 FX Brokers..46
   7.2 Types of Order...49
   7.3 Rand Volatility 53
   7.4 FX Broker Selection 55
   7.5 Foreign Exchange Controls..................................56
8. Rental Accommodation..............................57
   8.1 The Rental Contract..58
9. Removals 61
   9.1 Scope of Removals 63

- 9.2 Shipping Options 65
- 9.3 Customs Duties 66
- 9.4 Permanent Import of a Car 66
- 9.5 Estimated Removal Costs 67
- 10. Car Hire 68
  - 10.1 Excess Car Hire Insurance 68
  - 10.2 International Driving Permit (IDP) 69
- 11. Flights and Travel Insurance 71
  - 11.1 Flights 71
  - 11.2 Travel Insurance 72
- 12. Miscellaneous 73
  - 12.1 Car Navigation System 73
  - 12.2 Winter Temperatures 73
  - 12.3 eBook Readers 74

Part 3: On Arrival 75
- 13. Telecommunications 76
  - 13.1 Mobile Phones 76
  - 13.2 VOIP Phones 77
- 14. Tax 78
  - 14.1 Am I Tax Resident in South Africa? 78
  - 14.2 Am I Tax Resident in the UK? 80
  - 14.3 Why is this Important? 82
  - 14.4 Other Sources of Income 83

14.5 Capital Gains Tax (CGT) 86

14.6 Inheritance Tax (Estate Tax) 87

14.7 Other Tax Questions 88

15. UK Pensions 89

15.1 Private Pension 89

15.2 State Pension 90

16. Health Care 91

16.1 General Practitioners 91

16.2 Prescriptions and Chronic Medication 92

16.3 Pharmacist Services 92

17. Buying a Car 93

17.1 Traffic Register Number 93

17.2 Vehicle Registration 95

17.3 Annual Licence Fee 95

17.4 Annual Vehicle Inspection 96

17.5 Insurance 97

17.6 Cost of Purchasing a Car 98

18. Buying Property 100

18.1 Property Price Trends 100

18.2 Gated vs. Residential Area Living 103

18.3 Property Options 106

18.4 Property Marketing and Purchase Costs 110

18.5 Other Considerations 112

18.6 The Purchasing Process 113

19. Wills 116

   19.1 Immovable vs. Movable Objects 116

   19.2 Definition of Domicile 117

   19.3 Dying in South Africa without a Will 118

   19.4 Will Services 118

   19.5 Joint Wills 120

20. Miscellaneous 121

   20.1 South African Post Office (SAPO) 121

   20.2 Bank Charges 122

   20.3 Local Credit Cards 123

   20.4 Driving Licences 123

   20.5 Post Office Box 125

   20.6 TV Licence 125

   20.7 Informing the UK Government on Arrival 126

Appendices 127

   Appendix 1: Useful Links 128

      1.1 Foreign Exchange Currency Brokers 128

      1.2 Immigration Agents 128

      1.3 South African Banks 129

      1.4 Mobile Phone Networks 129

      1.5 Medical Aid Schemes 129

      1.6 Medical Aid Gap Insurance 130

- 1.7 Dental Insurance 130
- 1.8 Medical Aid Brokers 130
- 1.9 Car Insurance Underwriters 130
- 1.10 Real Estate Agents/Web Sites 131

Appendix 2: Chronic Medical Conditions 132

Appendix 3: Medical Aid Terminology 134

- 3.1 Waiting Period 134
- 3.2 Prescribed Minimum Benefits (PMB) 134
- 3.3 Late Joiners 135
- 3.4 Medical Scheme Tariff 136
- 3.5 Designated Service Provider 137
- 3.6 Gap Cover 137
- 3.7 Hospital Plan 138
- 3.8 Day to Day Benefits 138
- 3.9 Medical Savings Account 138
- 3.10 Threshold Benefits 139

Appendix 4: Day to Day Health Care Costs 140

- 4.1 Health Care Professional Fees 140
- 4.2 Diagnostic Tests and Lab Costs 140
- 4.3 Pharmacist Activities 141

Final Thoughts 142

Preface

My wife and I have enjoyed many holidays in South Africa over a long period of time. However, as a retirement destination, it has always been discounted, largely due to the crime statistics. Nevertheless, in March 2016 we decided to return once again, and say a final goodbye before moving to warmer climes. One of the holiday activities was a visit to Robben Island, where the former president Nelson Mandela was imprisoned for 18 of his 27 year incarceration. This involved a sea crossing during which we were seated next to a British lady who had emigrated some years earlier.

During the crossing, we fell into conversation, where she enthusiastically compared and contrasted her life in the UK with that in South Africa. She clearly had no regrets, and by the end of the crossing, it was clear that South Africa should once again appear on our list for further consideration. Thus, this story begins.

Within this book a number of costs are specified; these are all correct as of 2017. Typically, in-country costs are quoted in Rand and for the benefit of our UK readers are frequently converted into GBP. For this, an exchange rate of R16.8 to the GBP is used. As I write this in late October 2017 the exchange rate has fallen to R18.0 to the GBP, therefore the costs in GBP terms are overstated by 7%. Welcome to the volatile Rand!

Acknowledgments

To my wife for her constant love, support and encouragement.

To my parents whose sacrifices made all this possible.

Finally, to my readers who make all this worthwhile.

Part 1 - Why South Africa

1. Why South Africa?

Retiring to South Africa has many merits, from the friendliness of its people, through to its stunning scenery. However, we have cherry picked some of the highlights that we believe deserve consideration.

1.1 Climate

South Africa is a vast country, some five times larger than the UK in area, with its climate being influenced by both its topography and the currents of the Atlantic and Indian oceans. The result of all this is that the climatic conditions range from Mediterranean in the Western Cape to temperate in the interior plateau, and subtropical in the north-east. A small area in the Northern Cape even has a desert climate.

The Mediterranean climate of the Western Cape, combined with English being widely spoken, makes it a popular destination for retirees. Since South Africa is located in the southern hemisphere, the seasons are the opposite to what you would expect in the UK with the spring, summer, autumn and winter starting in September, December, March and June respectively. Because of this, the climate of the UK and the Western Cape can only really be compared on a seasonal basis. Hence, the graphs below compare the climate in London and Cape Town in the Western Cape in terms of temperature, rainfall and sunlight. The x-axis on each graph refers to the first, second and third month of each season. Thus 'Winter 1' refers to December in the UK compared to June in Cape Town etc.

1 WHY SOUTH AFRICA?

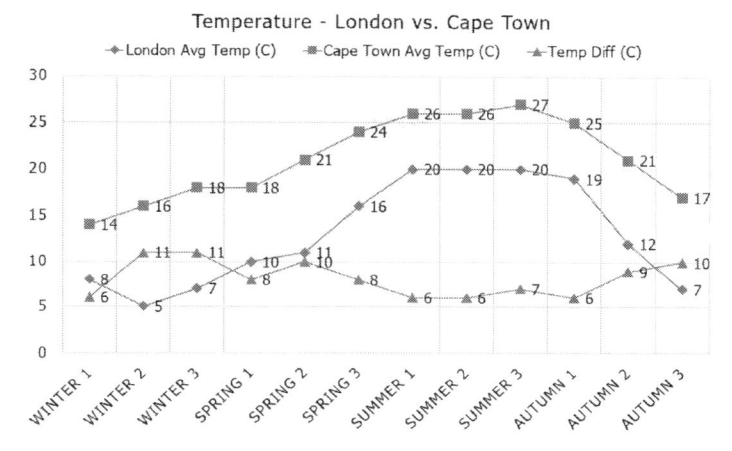

Temperature - London vs. Cape Town

As can be seen from the above graph the temperature, see 'Temp Dev', is typically on average some 8 degrees warmer than the corresponding London temperature. For most of the year, you can have breakfast out on the patio and the Summer temperatures are moderated by low humidity and are seldom oppressively hot. Thus, outdoor swimming pools are common, providing a minimum of a five-month swimming season, which can be inexpensively extended to 9 months a year by using solar heating.

Rainfall - London vs. Cape Town

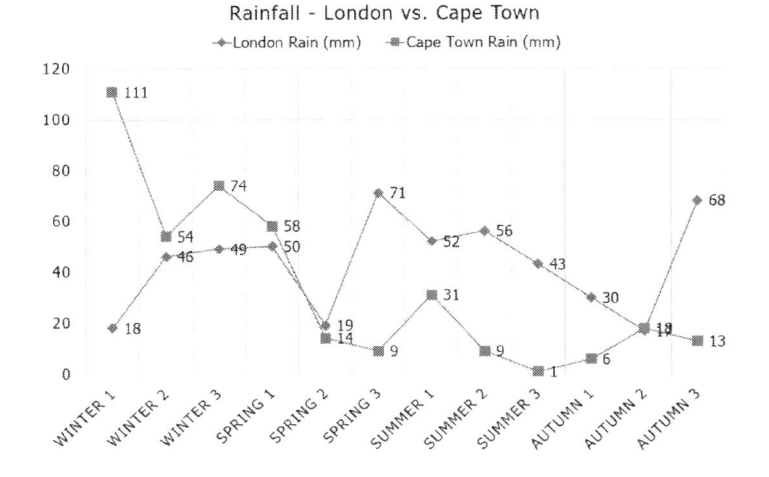

This graph shows that unlike the UK, the rain is more concentrated in the Winter. During this period the rain can be very heavy and extend over several days. Thereafter, it will clear giving way to blue skies and sunshine. However, outside the winter and early spring periods, the rain is significantly lower than the UK. Overall the annual rainfall is around 20% less than you would experience in the UK.

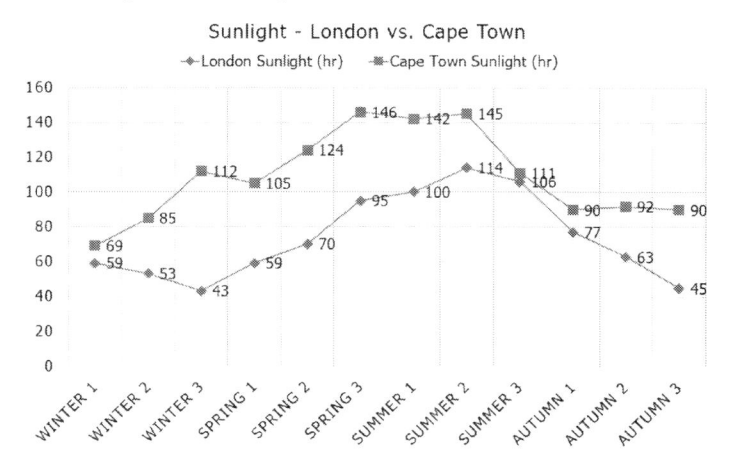

Sunlight - London vs. Cape Town

Here is where you would notice the most difference. On an annual basis, Cape Town enjoys 50% more sunlight hours than London, and that means lovely blue skies. It is particularly evident in Winter, where that ratio can rise to 100%.

Winds

Between September and March, the Western Cape province can be subject to a dry south-easterly wind. Although the wind blows over a wide area, it is notorious, especially in and around the Cape Peninsula, where it can be unpleasantly strong and irritating. Capetonians also call it 'the South-Easter'. It is usually accompanied by fair weather. However, occasionally it can bring heavy rain. Under such circumstances, it is known as 'Black South-Easter'. When purchasing property, it may be beneficial to consider its orientation to ensure the outside areas are protected from this wind.

Other snippets of weather trivia for Cape Town are:

- Driest months are January, February, March, November and December.
- On average, the warmest month is January.
- On average, the coolest month is August.
- June is the wettest month.

In conclusion, the Mediterranean climate allows us to have more fun outside, whether it is on the golf course, enjoying time by the pool or just walking in the sun.

1.2 Language

South Africa is a multilingual society with eleven official languages with many people speaking at least one language over and above their home language. Almost all young people can speak English or Afrikaans. As can be seen from the table below, even if English is not the first language it is still widely spoken or understood.

English Literacy

Ref.	Provinces	English First Language	English Spoken
1.	Western Cape	20%	Understood and spoken by most
2.	Eastern Cape	4%	Understood and spoken by many
3.	Northern Cape	0%	Understood by most
4.	Gauteng	13%	Understood and spoken by most
5.	Free State	0%	Main business language
6.	North West	0%	Understood and spoken by many
7.	KwaZulu-Natal	13%	Understood and spoken by most
8.	Limpopo	0%	Main business language
9.	Mpumalanga	0%	Understood and spoken by most

1.3 Permanent Right to Reside

Anybody retiring abroad is likely to invest in the country by purchasing a property. It may seem reasonable that they should have the right to reside permanently in that country, and make personal use of their investment. In reality, they are completely unrelated. Today, within the EU we are very fortunate in that we have the privilege to reside in any member state, accepting that the current situation may change with Brexit.

In other countries, you may not be so fortunate. For example, in New Zealand, assuming you don't have at least NZ $3M to invest and you don't have a family to join, then you will be limited to a temporary retirement visa. This is only applicable if you are 66 years or older and valid for two years. This visa requires you to meet financial requirements in terms of funds to invest, live on, as well as an annual income combined with an acceptable health insurance. Although this visa may be renewed indefinitely, there will come a time when they may revise the requirements upwards, your health or your investments decline and your visa will lapse. The requirements for Australia are not dissimilar.

Clearly, as you become older you are seen as less desirable, unless you are wealthy.

However, one point of difference in South Africa is that it offers both a temporary retirement visa and perhaps more importantly, a permanent retirement permit and the only qualifying financial requirement is having a more modest income or an equivalent investment portfolio which would generate such an income. This is discussed in more detail in section 3.

1.4 Income Tax-Friendly

South Africa has a progressive tax system, with a relatively low age dependent annual threshold (R117,300, £6982 at age 65). Thereafter, there is a progressive rate starting at 18% rising to 45%. As it stands, it would be difficult to describe the above arrangements as income tax-friendly.[1]

However, if you dig a bit deeper, you will find that income derived from a foreign pension scheme is not taxable. Let's just say that again. Assuming you are tax resident in South Africa, then income derived from a foreign pension scheme e.g. UK state pension, workplace pension, SIPP etc. will not be taxed. This is discussed in more detail in section 14.3 Tax.

---

[1] Further information can be found at SARS (South African Revenue Service), specifically http://www.sars.gov.za/Tax-Rates.

1.5 Extensive Expatriate Community

The latest UN data for 2015 shows that 4.9M people from the UK have migrated overseas. The table below lists the top destinations where the immigrant population is from the UK. What may be a surprise to many people is that South Africa takes the fourth position, ahead of all other European countries. Thus, you will find a significant expatriate community.

UK Emigration 2015

Ref.	Country	UK Emigration[2]
1.	Australia	1,289,396
2.	United States	714,999
3.	Canada	607,377
4.	South Africa	318,536
5.	Spain	308,821
6.	New Zealand	265,014
7.	Ireland	254,761
8.	France	185,344
9.	Germany	103,352
10.	Italy	64,986
11.	Channel Islands	59,380

---

[2] Data available from the UN Population Division - International Migration. Only those countries where the estimated UK immigrant population is greater than 30,000 are shown. (http://www.un.org/en/development/desa/population/)

1 WHY SOUTH AFRICA?

A much more difficult question to answer is what is the size of the retired UK population in South Africa? When a person migrates to another country no reasons are recorded. For an answer to this question, we must turn to the UK Department of Works and Pensions, and specifically ask how many people abroad are taking their state pension? Their response for the top fifteen countries is detailed below. This time South Africa is in the tenth position, but is still ahead of Cyprus, Portugal, Malta and Greece. Unfortunately, this underestimates the number of UK retirees, as you must have already reached state pensionable age and be taking your pension. Hence, those who retire earlier are excluded.

Pensioners in Receipt of UK State Pension – 2017

Ref.	Country	Number of UK Pensions[3]
1.	Australia	244,358
2.	Canada	143,802
3.	United States	138,159
4.	Ireland	134,840
5.	Spain	108,135
6.	France	66,864
7.	New Zealand	65,837
8.	Germany	43,076
9.	Italy	36,763
10.	South Africa	36,114
11.	Cyprus	18,572
12.	Switzerland	11,759
13.	Portugal	10,758
14.	Malta	6,485
15.	Greece	6,032

You can be confident that should you decide to retire to South Africa, you are not alone, as it is already home to a significant expatriate community.

---

[3] Data sourced from the UK Department of Work and Pensions based on pensioners claiming the state pension as of February 2017 (https://stat-xplore.dwp.gov.uk/webapi/jsf/login.xhtml)

1.6 Medical Facilities

As we get older we become more aware of the importance of having access to high quality medical facilities. Within the private sector, South Africa can offer first class healthcare in over 200 hospitals, which will rival, and in some cases, exceed what you can expect in the UK. All this comes at a cost, which is probably about one third of the equivalent private cost in the UK. Thus, private medical insurance or medical aid, see section 4, is highly recommended.

1.7 Domestic Help

From May 2018 the national minimum wage will be set at R20 per hour (£1.19 per hr), hardly a living wage, but a step in the right direction. However, for the retiree, it allows him to employ domestics or gardeners to do some of those more time consuming and heavier chores, freeing up more time for leisurely pursuits.

2. Why Not?

Unfortunately, nothing is ever perfect and South Africa still has a number of challenges, with corruption being one of the most destructive. This leads to social inequality and ultimately, crime. Many of our friends have lived in South Africa for their whole lives and the worst they have experienced is somebody stealing a pack of beer out of their car after leaving it unlocked or perhaps having their handbag snatched when they were on holiday, not in South Africa, but in London. Nevertheless, it would be remiss not to highlight the negatives.

2.1 Corruption

One, which may not be obvious to the visitor or retiree is corruption. Many of the country's leaders have come to office with an 'anti-corruption ticket' but have failed to live up to their pledges. One measure of corruption, or more precisely the perception of corruption is available from Transparency International[4], which in 2016 ranked South Africa 64 out of 176 countries. Perhaps globally this is a reasonable score and can be compared with the UK in 10th place, Spain 41st and Greece coming in the 69th position. Nevertheless, it is disappointing to note that the score hasn't significantly changed over the last four years. There is increasing evidence that the population wants to see change. The current leader, Jacob Zuma, is stepping down from his role as both the leader of the ANC and South Africa's president in late 2017 and 2019 respectively. One hopes that the newly elected leaders will be more effective at fighting corruption.

In addition to corruption, you will also hear the term 'State Capture'. This is where powerful and influential individuals attempt to influence outcomes by installing their own compliant management or even boards in state owned enterprises. The consequence of this is that such companies are more likely to place commercial contracts to the benefit of

---

[4] See: http://www.transparency.org

their sponsor rather than the enterprise. Ultimately, this results in poor value for money for the consumer. A report on state capture has been published which alleges improper and unethical conduct by both politicians and businesses. The result of this is that the President has committed himself to establishing a commission of inquiry. However, only time will tell if it results in any improvements.

In reality, the retiree is unlikely to notice it beyond some of the newspaper headlines.

2.2 Crime

Probably the greatest blight that South Africans experience is one of crime. Using murder as an example, South Africa is one of the more dangerous countries in the world. Looking at the latest available homicide rates (murders per 100,000 inhabitants) it can be seen that the South African murder rate is 37 times higher than the equivalent UK rate as detailed below, although a long way short of El Salvador.

Ref.	Country	Murder Rate[5]
1.	UK	0.92
2.	United States	4.88
3.	Brazil	26.74
4.	South Africa	34.27
5.	Jamaica	43.21
6.	El Salvador	108.64

As with all statistics, the devil is in the detail. Research has shown that murders are often not premeditated, but take place when an argument leads to physical assault. Most victims are

---

[5] Murder rate data obtained from Wikipedia
(https://en.wikipedia.org/wiki/List_of_countries_by_intentional_homicide_rate)

killed by acquaintances, friends or family members during disputes that are often fuelled by alcohol. The risk of becoming a victim of crime substantially depends on your race, gender, age, economic status and where you live.

The uncomfortable truths are:

- Gang violence claims many lives.
- Serious crimes are mainly experienced in low-income areas and townships.
- Almost half of the victims of sexual offences know their perpetrator.

Thus, there are vast differences in risk between areas. Half of South Africa's murders in 2014/15 occurred in only 12.3% of police precincts. On the other hand, one in five police stations in predominantly affluent metro and rural areas and towns has a murder rate of less than 12 per 100,000 with just over 10% of police precincts having a murder rate of zero. Another example is that the murder rate in Cape Town is 80% greater than the national average. However, almost two-thirds of the Cape Town murders took place in just ten of the sixty police station precincts in the city. As high as the murder rate is, murder accounts for less than 3% of all violent crime.

Unfortunately, crime is an issue that is not easy to address. It is argued by some that the current levels of crime arise as there is a general lack of respect for the law. This stems back to apartheid where many of the laws were unjust and were subsequently applied unfairly. In addition, the security forces, particularly the police, were used by the state to ensure that all South Africans lived in fear of the state, regardless of their race. Today, attitudes towards the law are demonstrated in small things such as the high number of people who drive without seat belts and who drive under the influence of drugs or alcohol.

There is no quick fix and it will take time to restore confidence in the rule of law. Until that time, the risks can be mitigated, but never eliminated, by carefully selecting where you live.

2.3 Frozen UK State Pension

If you retire to any countries in the European Economic area and selected other countries, e.g. Gibraltar, Switzerland and the US, your pension will be indexed as it is in the UK.

Unfortunately, if you retire to Canada, South Africa, New Zealand, Austria and many ex-Commonwealth countries, it is not indexed. This issue affects 550,000 British pensions representing about half the pensioners living overseas.

This means that rather than the annual uprating received by UK pensioners, their pension is frozen at the level first received for the rest of their life abroad. In practice, this means that their state pension decreases in real terms year-on-year. For example, a pensioner aged 90, who has lived in a frozen country all his retirement would now still get a state pension of just £43.60 per week. If he had lived in the UK he would receive £113.10.

It is generally accepted that the current policy is unjust, as we all contribute into the state pension but the amount we get out is dependent on where we choose to reside. There is an all-party parliamentary group (APPG[6]) on Frozen British Pensions that exists to bring together parliamentary supporters of the case to unfreeze such pensions. However, in view of the state of the UK finances, resolution of this discriminatory practice may take some time.

---

[6] See http://frozenbritishpensions.org/the-problem

Part 2 – Before Departure

3. Visas

Holders of a British passport may travel to South Africa but not work, for a stay of up to 90 days. This 90 days period may be extended by a District or Regional Office of the Department of Home Affairs for an additional 90 days, providing an application for an extension is made 30 days prior to the expiry of the original permit. The approval of such an extension is discretionary and hence not guaranteed.

It is assumed that the retiree does not have a South African spouse or relatives and therefore there are three options available:

- Retired person's visa.
- Financially independent permit.
- Retired person's permanent residence permit.

Before progressing further, it is worth noting the difference between 'Visa' and 'Permit'. The former refers to a temporary permission for a fixed period whilst the latter is for life. Unfortunately, within the literature, the terms are often used interchangeably.

3.1 Retired Person's Visa

This is for a period of four years and is required for each person, with each person having to satisfy the conditions in his/her own right. No age restriction is placed on this visa but it doesn't allow the applicant to work within South Africa. This visa requires the following supporting documentation, with all time sensitive documents dated within six months of your application, unless otherwise stated:

Police Clearance Certificate

This is required for all persons over eighteen from all countries where you have resided for more than 12 months. For the UK this can be obtained online from the Acro Criminal Records Office.[7]

For this you will need:

- Proof of current address - 2 different types of proof e.g. bank statements, utility bills or phone bill etc.
- Passport style photograph.
- Copy of your passport.
- Email address.
- Address history - for the last 10 years.
- Endorser details - friend, employer but not family.
- UK National Insurance and Driving Licence number.

Once you have all the above, you can simply complete the online application form and upload images of the required documents. The standard service takes about 10 working days and costs £45. There is also a premium service available if required at a cost of £80. Things become slightly more complicated if you have lived abroad for more than one year. Under such circumstances, you will have to contact the appropriate consulate to request a certificate of good character, for which they may require your fingerprints to be taken using the older ink method.[8]

---

[7] See: https://www.acro.police.uk/police_certificates.aspx
[8] Today in the UK most fingerprints are electronically scanned, however, one starting point would be:
(www.met.police.uk/request/your-fingerprints/).

3 VISAS

Radiological Report
You will need a report to confirm that a radiologist has examined you by X-ray and you have no signs of pulmonary tuberculosis. Pregnant women and children under 12 years are exempt from this requirement. The easiest way is to go along to your nearest private hospital for the examination; cost is circa £80. The form that must be completed is BI-806.[9]

Medical Report
You will need a medical report from your local GP relating to your general health, which includes any medical conditions that you may be suffering from. Typically, this will cost circa £70. The form that must be completed is BI-811.[10]

Authenticated Birth Certificate
The requirements in this area appear to have changed recently. Previously a certified copy of the birth certificate was required. However, it now appears that it is only required in respect of dependent children joining the applicant. If required, the certificate must now be authenticated by means of an Apostille from the issuing country. The recommendation here would be to check the latest requirements.

Marriage Certificate
This requirement has also changed slightly, as it must now be authenticated by means of an Apostille from the issuing country. Assuming a UK certificate, then this will cost £35.[11]

---

[9] Available from www.southafricahouseuk.com/documents/rdiological_bi-806.pdf
[10] Available from www.southafricahouseuk.com/documents/mdcal_bi-811.pdf
[11] See 'Get your document legalised (www.gov.uk/get-document-legalised)' for further information.

Bank Statements
Bank statements for the last 3 months, not older than 7 days. These must be stamped by the bank or supported by a verification letter from the bank. The easiest method is just to print them out and take them to the local branch for stamping.

Divorce Decree
If appropriate.

Passport Photographs
Two required.

Financial Requirements
To meet the necessary financial requirements, the applicant will need to show that he/see receive a monthly income of at least R37,000 (£2,200) through one of the following ways.

- The R37,000 must originate from abroad and can be shown through a pension, irrevocable annuity or a retirement account; or
- The R37,000 can also be shown through a combination of assets such as rental income, investment income etc.

The right to a pension at some future date is insufficient. This is a grey area, but one interpretation is that it is acceptable that you currently have a right to such a pension but have chosen not to take it. An alternative method is that since the visa is only valid for 4 years, then you need to demonstrate that you have savings equivalent to 48 months * R37,000 (£105,700) through bank statements. The financial requirement is per applicant and must be confirmed by a South African chartered accountant.

Yellow Fever Vaccination Certificate

A yellow fever vaccination certificate is required to be submitted if you have travelled through or intend travelling through a yellow fever endemic area prior to submitting your residence application. Generally, this is not applicable.

The Application Form

Having assembled all the supporting documentation you are now ready to complete the application form, DHA 1738 Form 8.[12]

Within this form you must:

- Select the required category - Retired Person's Visa.
- Complete sections 1 .. 5.
- Section 6 - Maintenance/Deportation - Make reference to the chartered accountant's certificate confirming that you meet the financial requirements.
- Section 7 - Reference your spouse.
- Complete sections 8 .. 10, remembering to sign the declaration.
- Complete the summary table which identifies the supporting documentation which is provided as part of this application.
- Put a diagonal line through all the remaining sections for the different classes of visa other than the category for which you are applying.

---

[12] Available from www.southafricahouseuk.com/documents/dha1738form8.pdf

The Application Process

You now have a completed application with supporting documentation. What do you do next? Assuming you are based in the UK, you will now have to schedule an interview appointment at your nearest VFS Global Centre and pay the necessary fee (£40) and the courier cost of returning your passport (£14.95). The centres are located in London, Manchester and Edinburgh.[13]

On the day of your appointment ensure that you take the:

- Completed application form with all supporting documentation.
- Originals of all documentation.
- Appointment letter.

As part of the appointment you will be required to:

- Surrender your passport whilst the visa is appended, this will typically take 6-8 weeks, during which you will be unable to travel overseas.
- Pay the visa application fee (£35).

The interview, which will take around 30 minutes, is nothing to be concerned about as it is largely an exercise in reviewing the paperwork. Once you have your temporary retirement visa it can be renewed every four years, providing you can still satisfy the requirements.

---

[13] See www.vfsglobal.com/southafrica/uk/Schedule_an_Appointment.html

Should I Use an Immigration Agent?
One of the challenges with the immigration process is the South African Immigration Act. Although the South African Immigration Act is in essence fairly straight-forward, it is also open to varying interpretations. Through constant changes in approach and policy on how the Act should be enforced, officials at the South African Department of Home Affairs, South African Consulates, High Commissions and Embassies tend to offer varying and inconsistent guidance and process applications differently. It is certainly possible to adopt a DIY approach. However, one of the challenges is getting the necessary financial statement. If you don't have access to the necessary chartered accountant, and it must be a South African registered accountant, then the local Tax Shop[14] may be able to help. Alternatively, you may opt to use an Immigration Agent. Generally, they will complete the application form on your behalf, provide the necessary financial statement and answer queries as they arise. Nevertheless, you will still be responsible for obtaining all the other supporting documentation. This level of service comes at a cost as detailed below.

---

[14] Tax Shop - Celia McGuinness (franschhoek@taxshop.co.za - +27 21 876 2676) has previously been very helpful in preparing the necessary financial statement.

DIY vs. Immigration Agent based on a Joint Application

Ref	Description	DIY	Immigration Agent[15]
1.	UK Police Clearance	£90	£90
2.	Radiological Report	£160	£160
3.	Medical Report	£140	£140
4.	Marriage Certification Authentication	£35	£35
5.	Financial Statement SA Chartered Accountant	£150	
6.	VFS Global Fees • Appointment • Passport Courier	£80 £30	£80 £30
7.	Visa Application Fee	£70	£70
8.	Immigration Agent Includes accountant fee		£800
	Total Cost:	**£755**	**£1,405**

If you choose to use an immigration agent then there are a number available, see appendix 1. Many of these services are legitimate and their agents are very knowledgeable, helpful and can take much of the frustration away. Unfortunately, there are others who might be best described as 'fly-by-night' businesses which create more frustration than they are worth. You should always ensure that any agent you select is a registered immigration practitioner or lawyer.

---

[15] Immigration Agents - Generally an immigration agent will charge full price for the first applicant and apply a 50% reduction for the second applicant.

On a personal note, Intergate Immigration has been used and was found to be excellent.[16]

3.2 Financial Independent Permit 27(F)

Applying for permanent residence through the 'Financially Independent' category is generally used as an alternative to applying through the Retired Person's category if a person does not have the required monthly lifelong income for the Retired Person's category, but has the necessary capital and net worth. Unfortunately, it does require the applicant to pay a fee of R120,000 to the South African government and therefore in many cases it is not the preferred approach. This fee is only payable if the application is successful.

The requirements share many similarities with those of the Retirement Visa. However, in this case, only one application is made and the spouse may be appended to it. In summary, the requirements are:

- Completed on-line DHA-947.
- Valid passport.
- Passport photograph.
- Marriage certificate.
- Divorce decree.
- Birth certificate.
- Police certificate.
- Radiological report.
- Medical report.
- Yellow fever vaccination certificate.

---

[16] See: www.intergate-immigration.com

In addition to the above, a financial statement is required that proves the applicant has a prescribed minimum net worth (R12M, £714K). There is no requirement for these funds to be brought into the country.

The application fees are:

- VFS Global fee: R1,350 (£80)
- DHA (Dept. Home Affairs): R1,520 (£90)

The average processing time is in the range 8 - 10 months but may be much longer.

3.3 Retired Person's Permanent Permit 27(E)

The requirements are almost identical to the financial independent permit, with the sole exception of the financial requirements. In this case, the financial requirements are to provide proof that the applicant has either:

- The right to a pension or irrevocable annuity or retirement account which will give such foreigner a prescribed minimum payment per month (R37,000) for the rest of his or her life. Or
- Has a minimum prescribed net worth per month (R37,000) realising from the combination of assets.

There is no requirement to pay the application fee of R120,000 to the South African government.

Costs for a DIY Joint Application from within South Africa

Ref	Description	DIY
1.	UK Police Clearance	£90 (R1,500)
2.	Radiological Report	R1,176 (£70)
3.	Medical Report	R700 (£42)
4.	Certified Marriage and Birth Certificate [17]	R0 (£0)
5.	Financial Statement SA Chartered Accountant	R1,730 (£103)
6.	VFS Global Fee	R1,350 (£80)
7.	Visa Application Fee	R1,520 (£90)
	Total Cost:	**R7,976 (£475)**

3.4 Should I Apply for a Visa or Permit?

The various types are not mutually exclusive. It is not uncommon for a retiree to apply simultaneously for both a Retired Person's Visa and Permit.

The major differences are:

- Processing time. A visa will be processed in 8 weeks compared to 8 - 10 months or even longer for a permit.
- Economic restrictions. A retirement visa does not allow a person to work whilst there are no such restrictions on a permit.
- Import duties. A permit holder is able to import a car into South Africa duty-free, providing it has been owned by him for the last 12 months.
- Time period. A permit is for life whilst a visa needs to be renewed every four years.

---

[17] Documents may be certified free of charge by taking the original and copy along to the local police station.

- Financial requirements. The requirements for a visa may be easier to satisfy.
- If you apply for a Permit, then it could be interpreted as an intent to settle permanently in South Africa. Thus, on arrival, you could potentially be seen as ordinarily tax resident. Depending upon your own circumstances, this may be undesirable, see section 14 Tax.

The costs of obtaining either a retired person's visa or permit are broadly similar. If the applicant can meet the financial requirements for a permit and can tolerate its extended processing times, then the permit may the preferred approach. One other consideration is that requirements can change. You may be able to satisfy the requirements today but who knows about tomorrow. If you are intending to purchase a property in South Africa, then having a permanent right to reside is highly desirable.

One hybrid approach is for one spouse to apply for the Permit whilst the other spouse applies for the Visa. This potentially allows you to transfer assets between each other to minimise your tax liability.

4. Health Care

The South African health system is split into both a private and public sector. The private sector offers world class treatment and as such it attracts in excess of 300,000 annual health tourists for medical treatment. Some 60% of all medical personnel work in the private sector, which is accessible by only 16% of the population. Unfortunately, medical services in the public sector are understaffed and underfunded and are significantly less capable. The government aspires to transform the ailing public sector by introducing a new National Health Insurance Scheme (NHI); however, funding for this new initiative remains challenging.

Consequently, anybody emigrating to South Africa should have a suitable plan to allow access to the private sector. Fortunately, a number of options are available:

- Private Medical Insurance
- Hospital Cash Plans
- Medical Aid

4.1 Private Medical Insurance

These are available from both local insurers within South Africa and large international companies such as Bupa, Cigna and Pacific Prime. One of the issues with international insurances, but could also be argued as a strength, is that the insurance provides global coverage, whereas in South Africa medical costs are lower than international levels, and this isn't always reflected in the premium. The other challenge around private medical insurance is how pre-existing conditions and chronic conditions are covered together with the inevitable increases in premiums as we age. We may be perfectly healthy now, and then develop a condition, which although initially covered, then becomes a pre-existing condition on annual policy renewal, at which point cover may be restricted or indeed denied, or premiums significantly increased.

4.2 Hospital Cash Plans

These may be confused with medical aid, however, they are not and should be seen as an insurance policy which pays a cash sum out based on the duration of hospitalisation. Thus, there is no relationship between the cost of treatment received and the sum paid out. These types of plans are aimed at giving the individual extra cash on hand for additional costs and to cover partially the loss of income during a hospital stay. They may appear to be inexpensive and hence attractive, but the coverage is very limited.

4.3 Medical Aid

Medical aid is specific to South Africa and is regulated by the Medical Schemes Act (1998). They are essentially non-profit organisations that belong to their members. The purpose of medical aid is to ensure that you are able to pay for treatment from either family practitioners or whilst in hospital. This section uses some terminology which is specific to medical aid. These terms are defined in appendix 3. Medical aid schemes must:

- Operate on a not for profit basis.
- Cover you for those chronic conditions defined in appendix 2.
- Cannot decline your application, regardless of your age or medical history. However, they can impose a late joiner penalty and exclusion periods around existing conditions, see appendix 3.
- Provide cover for 270 conditions according to prescribed minimum benefits PMB).
- Your membership can only be terminated on grounds of failing to pay your membership fees, committing fraud, or non-disclosure of material information. Thus, when completing an application form, it is important not to withhold any medical information.

Currently, there are some 22 open medical aid schemes open in South Africa which between them offer around 140 plans. Such plans can be categorised into four major groups:

- Hospital only plans
- Hospital + Saver
- Hospital + Saver Plus
- Comprehensive plans

Hospital Only Plans
These provide for in-hospital cover only, with the exception of chronic illness and PMBs (Prescribed Minimum Benefits) which are provided by all registered medical aids. They may also provide partial cover for specialised scans such as MRI and CT.

Hospital + Saver
The member's contribution is used to fund both the risk element (hospital) and an individual saving account. The saving element is used to fund day to day health needs such as visits to family practitioners or dentists. Should the savings account become exhausted then the member will be directly responsible for funding the additional costs. Any surplus in the saving account at the end of the year will be rolled forward into the next year. Should the member decide to leave the scheme, then the balance in the saving account will be refunded to him.

Hospital + Saver Plus
This is similar to the above but includes threshold benefits. Initially, day to day benefits are paid from the medical savings account. Once this is exhausted the member will be required to pay any additional costs up to the self-payment gap. Once the self-payment gap has been breached, threshold benefits will start with any additional costs being paid by the scheme until a limit is reached. This provides a safety net against the member experiencing large day to day expenses.

Comprehensive Plans
This is similar to the Hospital + Saver Plus plan but in this case benefits above the threshold are unlimited.

Which Scheme/Plan is Right for Me?
This is largely determined by your attitude towards risk and perhaps your financial discipline. For example, do you insure everything in your house? Perhaps you only insure what you can't afford to replace or you have a legal requirement to insure. Do you insure your satellite box or take a view that if it fails you just source a replacement? It could be suggested that a good quality hospital plan is a necessity whilst a Hospital Plan + Saver only provides some additional financial management; in that they save your money on your behalf and then pay it back when required.

After deciding which group is right for you, then the next step is selecting the correct plan. The choice of plan is less critical, as every medical aid scheme allows its members to change the plan at the end of each year. In addition, some schemes will allow you to change your plan if you are diagnosed with a dreaded disease. However, you can't readily move between schemes for the first 24 months without being subject to further exclusion periods, although PMBs will still be covered, nor can you be members of more than one scheme at any one time.

The choice of scheme is not an easy one but fortunately, a company called GTC[18] carry out an annual medical aid survey and compare benefits and costs. They have compared the plans by considering both the plan's competitiveness (benefits vs. member contribution) together with other factors that may determine the sustainability of the plan, such as membership numbers and age distribution, financial stability and service

---

[18] GTC's 2017 medical aid survey can be accessed either from their main page or from http://www.gtc.co.za/wp-content/uploads/2017/07/gtc-mas-2017-a4-v21-single-page.pdf

levels to produce a composite score. Altogether, it is a very comprehensive piece of work and an excellent basis for informed decision making. Based on two adults, their top two recommendations for 2017 with monthly costs for two adults but excluding any late joiner penalties, which can be significant, typically an additional 50%-75%, for each of the above groups are as follows:

Recommended Medical Aid Schemes and Plans

Ref	Group	Scheme and Plan
1.	Hospital Only	Discovery - Essential Smart (R2,200) Genesis - Private Choice (R2,000)
2.	Hospital + Saver	Discovery - Essential Delta Saver (R3,963) Discovery - Classic Delta Saver (R3,083)
3.	Hospital + Saver Plus	Discovery - Essential Priority (R4,953) Discovery - Classic Priority (R5,658)
4.	Comprehensive	Momentum - Extender (R7,737) Discovery - Essential Delta Comprehensive (R7,184)

The above costs assume that the hospitals are selected from the schemes network. From these results, it is difficult to recommend anything other than Discovery as the medical aid scheme. One of the constraints imposed by the majority of the above recommendations is that the available hospitals are limited to their designated service provider (DSP). However, the DSP may provide poor coverage in your geographical area and thus the above may have to be tempered with that knowledge. If you are moving to the coastal areas, then one of Discovery's coastal plans should be considered. Discovery, through data analysis, has concluded that members living in the coastal areas are slightly healthier, and therefore they are able to offer slightly lower contributions and a wider hospital selection by restricting members to only using hospitals in the coastal region for planned admissions.

Before leaving the subject of medical aid, it is worth touching on the subject of gap cover. Gap cover is a relatively inexpensive short-term insurance product which compliments any medical aid. All medical aid schemes try to control their costs by introducing co-payments for selected procedures, requiring you to use designated service providers and limiting the rates at which medical personnel are reimbursed. Thus, in reality even with medical aid, you may be faced with a shortfall for which you would normally be responsible. However, gap insurance provides a means of addressing this shortfall.

If you are still struggling to decide whether a basic hospital plan or a more comprehensive solution should be selected, then appendix 4 has some examples of day to day health costs. One possible solution is to select a basic hospital plan. Ideally it should cover a wide range of procedures but perhaps with significant co-payments and then back that up with a comprehensive gap policy. Note that gap cover only addresses the shortfall where the medical aid covers the procedure. Hence, if there is no cover under the medical aid policy then there is no basis for a claim under the gap cover. Finally, if you select a basic hospital plan you may wish to consider a separate dental policy. These can be very inexpensive and can cover everything from basic dentistry right through to advanced procedures such as root canals, crowns and implants. Appendix 1 has a list of dental insurers.

Should You Get Medical Aid/Gap Insurance Before Arrival?
All medical aid will normally impose a 3-month exclusion period on new members with the possibility of a 12 month exclusion period on pre-existing conditions. Gap policies may also have exclusion periods. Thus, to ensure that you have full coverage on arrival you may wish to consider taking medical aid out in advance. However, regardless of any medical aid waiting periods, you are automatically covered for

emergencies as soon as the plan is taken out. The other consideration is the late joiner penalty, which is defined in appendix 3. This has a number of price breaks. For example, if you take medical aid out at age 59, without having any previous medical aid, the risk element of your contribution will be subject to a penalty of 50%. However, if you delay taking out aid until age 60, then the penalty will rise to 75% for the rest of your life. Thus, in some cases, it may be advisable to take out a low-cost policy early prior to departure to avoid such a penalty.

In order to take out medical aid you will require a South African:

- Bank account. Payments must be made by direct debits in Rand and thus credit cards are not acceptable.
- Mailing address.
- Telephone number.

Fortunately, all the above can be readily achieved. The policy may be taken out directly with the provider or alternatively you can go via a medical aid broker. There is no financial advantage in going direct and in some cases, the broker may allow you to use his address as the mailing address. Brokers are allowed to receive a commission of 3% of your total monthly contribution for their services up to a maximum of R75 plus VAT per month. This commission covers the initial introduction as well as providing on-going service. A good broker should be able to recommend a plan together with an associated gap policy as well as keeping you up to date with changes in the benefit structure. Personal experience suggests that some of the smaller brokers are prepared to offer a personal service and respond to questions whilst some of the larger firms lose interest as soon as you have taken the policy out. On a personal note, I would advise you to do your own research in respect of the medical scheme/plan. The reasoning is that brokers can only recommend schemes that they have an arrangement with and it is impractical to expect a broker to have detailed knowledge of the 22 open schemes and their various plans.

As stated earlier, one of the prerequisites for taking out a policy is having a South African mailing address. One simple solution is to take out a virtual office via Regus[19] or equivalent service, selecting only the professional address option. This seems to satisfy the requirements of the medical aid scheme which they will then use to send out your membership card. Once this has been received, then simply cancel your virtual office subscription.

4.4 Healthcare Costs and Inflation

Over the last 16 years, the average year-on-year increase of medical scheme contributions has been 7.6%. This is 1.9% higher than the CPI inflation. This is a worldwide phenomenon, which is driven by the high cost of medication, new medical technology, and in addition in South Africa, by the weakening exchange rate. Hence, when budgeting you should assume a cost escalation which is both slightly greater than the CPI and the typical investment rates you could get at the banks, currently circa 7%.

4.5 Pre-Existing Medical Conditions

Medical aid, but not insurance, cannot refuse your application based on your medical history. However, they can impose exclusion periods of up to one year. Should you have any medical records then bring them with you, as the scheme may request them to support your application and potentially minimise any exclusion period that they may otherwise apply.

---

[19] Regus, see www.regus.co.za

5. Telecommunications

5.1 Land Lines

South Africa may be physically a great distance from the UK but there is no reason to lose contact with your family and friends. When you relocate you will almost certainly have the availability of an Internet connection and although it may lack the speed that we are accustomed to in the UK, it is certainly adequate for our communications needs. A few years ago, a piece of disruptive technology called VOIP (Voice over Internet Protocol) was introduced. Initially, it was used by the technical geeks but has now matured into mainstream use. It provides an alternative way of making phone calls cheaply or even for free. In many cases, it is used to communicate between parties using their computers and appropriate headsets. However, we will describe how calls can be made from a VOIP enabled phone via the Internet to a conventional phone. For this capability we will need:

- VOIP enabled phone.
- Services of a VOIP provider.

VOIP Enabled Phone

Although calls can be made from an Internet connected computer via a headset it is perhaps not the most convenient arrangement. Manufacturers[20] have responded to this new need by developing VOIP enabled phones. These look like an existing DECT cordless phone consisting of a base station and a number of extensions. In the case of Siemens, the base station can be both plugged into a conventional telephone socket and your Internet router. One interesting difference is that with a conventional phone you are restricted to having only a single call at any one time. VOIP phones don't have this restriction so that it is perfectly possible that if you had two extensions you and your spouse could be having two completely separate conversations simultaneously.

VOIP Provider

Your selected VOIP provider provides you with a geographical phone number and will ensure that any calls made to that number are routed to your VOIP phone wherever it is located in the world. So, for example, suppose you select a UK VOIP provider, e.g. Voipfone[21], they would then assign you a UK number. Thus, suppose you are in the UK and your friends dial the assigned number, then the call will be routed via your VOIP provider to your VOIP enabled phone. The caller, assuming he is a BT customer, pays the standard BT charge for a UK call. Now, suppose you are located in South Africa. The caller makes the same call, which is routed and charged in the same manner as the previous call. Thus, when your VOIP number is called the cost is

---

[20] Siemens manufacture a range of VOIP enabled phones under the Gigaset brand name e.g. A540IP, SL450A and S650 etc. All are readily available from Amazon or your selected VOIP provider.
[21] Voipfone (www.voipfone.co.uk) is a well-established, award winning UK VOIP service provider. They enjoy an excellent reputation in terms of voice quality, system availability and customer service.

6 BANKING

independent of your physical location.

Let us also consider what happens when a VOIP call is initiated from South Africa via your UK geographical number to your family and friends in the UK. From a cost perspective it is just seen as a UK national call and again the cost is independent of your physical location.

One of the many advantages of a VOIP service is that such calls are significantly less expensive compared to using a conventional telecoms operator, such as BT or South African Telkom, as shown in the table below. In fairness, the table doesn't tell the whole story. If you have a BT call inclusive package then calls to a national UK number may be free. Your VOIP provider will also likely charge between £2-3 per month for the geographical number.

Call Charges

Ref	Call Description	Telecoms Operator	VOIP Provider
1.	Calling VOIP UK number from the UK	12 PPM[22] + 21p set-up fee (BT)	1.2 PPM (Voipfone)
2.	Calling a South Africa number from the UK	76 PPM + 21p set-up fee (BT)	9.6 PPM (Voipfone)
3.	Calling the UK whilst in South Africa	4 PPM (Telkom)	1.2 PPM (Voipfone)

Nevertheless, you can see that VOIP has many cost advantages and you can give your UK VOIP number out to your friends and family in the knowledge that they can use it and only incur standard BT call charges no matter where you are physically located. Hence, it can be both good and cheap to talk!

---

[22] PPM - Pence per Minute including VAT

Modern VOIP enabled phones are not limited to a single VOIP provider but in many cases, can support a maximum of 6. So, for example, in addition to your UK VOIP provider, you could also select a South African provider, e.g. SwitchTel[23]. They will issue you with a local South African number and thus any calls either to your UK or South African VOIP numbers will be routed to your phone anywhere in the world. When you initiate a call, you can decide whether to dial using your UK or SA VOIP accounts. Hence, calls to both UK and SA numbers will be charged at local rather than international rates. The one downside is that SwitchTel, without proof of a South African address, will initially be able to offer you only a non-geographical number. However, once you have a South African address, you can get the number changed to a geographical one. The advantage of having a South African VOIP number is that it allows you to take out Medical Aid prior to arrival since having a local number is a prerequisite.

Another alternative which you may wish to consider is Skype, which offers both calls to landlines and video conferencing facilities.[24]

5.2 Mobile Phones

Mobile phones are extensively used in South Africa, much more so than landlines and one very popular application is WhatsApp. One option you have here is to upgrade your mobile to one that is capable of supporting dual SIMS e.g. Motorola Moto G5. That way you can maintain your UK mobile number for WhatsApp application and also be able to install a South African SIM for in-country use. [25]

---

[23] SwitchTel is a leading VOIP provider in South Africa, see www.switchtel.co.za
[24] See www.skype.com/en
[25] See www.whatsapp.com

6. Banking

6.1 UK Banking

The first question to ask is whether you are going to retire to South Africa on a full-time basis, or are you going to maintain your UK address and act as 'swallows' and migrate according to the seasons? Unless you are very fortunate and able to maintain two separate properties you are going to lose your UK address. This can be positively advantageous when considering tax residency but this will be covered in section 14. However, one of the downsides is with the increased awareness of money laundering, you may struggle to open UK bank accounts once you have relocated. Hence, before relocating you should:

- Confirm that you can continue with your current banker once you have relocated and he is able to issue replacement debit cards etc. If your existing banker can't support you then consider switching to an alternative. However, if you are applying for a temporary visa, then you need to provide three months bank statements. Try to avoid switching banks during this period as it can cause confusion with your application.
- Open up any saving accounts that you may need and ensure they are comfortable with an address outside the UK. As an example, Sainsbury's bank requires a UK address, so once you lose your UK address, they will require you to close any accounts down.
- Consider a credit card that doesn't charge commission on foreign transactions.
- Most banks make extensive use of either a land-line or mobile telephone number for authentication purposes. Consider how this is going to work in the future and update your contact details if needed.

- Update your credit card provider with your travel plans to ensure they don't flag any South African transactions as fraudulent.

6.2 South African Banking

Do you need to set a bank account up prior to arrival? If you are intending to take Medical Aid out in advance, then the answer is a clear yes as it is a requirement. If that answer is no, then a local bank account becomes useful rather than a necessity. The advantages of setting up a bank account in advance are:

- Setting it up well in advance means that it is easier to deal with any issues before they become time critical.
- It allows you to buy local currency in advance and take advantage of exchange rates.
- Funds in a saving account can earn useful interest, currently 7.10% per annum.
- In some areas, South Africa is a cashless society and people avoid carrying large amounts due to the possibility of robbery. Hence, paying by a debit card is probably easier and safer.
- Paying rent and deposits is easier.

The only disadvantage is that you may start paying for banking services a little bit early and may have to pay for Fed Ex or equivalent to deliver your new plastic cards to the UK.

Joint Bank Accounts in South Africa

Joint bank accounts in the UK are relatively common but are no longer available in South Africa. A similar capability can be provided by the principal opening the account and then allow the spouse to access the account via a power of attorney. Under normal circumstances, this arrangement works well. However, should the principal die then there is a risk that as the power of attorney is no longer valid, then spousal access to the account may be denied. Thus, it may be appropriate that both parties open up their own accounts with each one having power of attorney over the other.

Which South African Bank?

In South Africa, there is a set of independent national benchmarks which are used to measure customer satisfaction of service providers. This considers such factors as customer experience, perceived quality, customer expectations, customer loyalty and complaints. This benchmark (SAcsi) applied to retail banks can be used as the basis for bank selection.

Retail Banking Scores - 2017

Ref	Bank	SAcsi Score
1.	Capitec	83.1
2.	FNB	81.3
3.	Nedbank	77.0
4.	Absa	74.2
5.	Standard Bank	71.9

The results would suggest that Capitec should be selected. Unfortunately, their savings interest rate (circa 5.1%) is significantly lower than that offered by FNB[26] (circa 7.1%) and therefore is probably not the best choice for those with significant funds to invest. Therefore, we would recommend FNB (First National Bank) and this has been confirmed by our own experience. Previously we were with Nedbank. This original account was set-up prior to our arrival in South Africa and Nedbank provided a very efficient on-boarding process during which we were assigned a dedicated relationship manager. However, on arrival, because of our non-resident status, we found that the branch could do very little for us and all requests had to go through this assigned manager. This we found to be very cumbersome, and hence the move to FNB.

Opening a South African Account from the UK
All the major banks maintain a non-residence centre to support the opening of banking facilities from outside the country. Typically, the following documentation is required:

- Certified copy of the photo page of your passport.
- Certified copy of your residence permit (if available).
- Proof of current address, e.g. utilities bill.
- Three months' bank statements from your previous countries bank, showing the activity on the account.
- A certificate of introduction from your previous countries bank, showing your personal details and signed by a bank official, with their name and contact number on the letter.

---

[26] See: www.fnb.co.za/foreign/non-resident-centre.html.
Email: nonres@fnb.co.za

It will also be necessary to complete the bank's:

- Application form.
- Foreign exchange questionnaire.
- Source of funds statement.
- Needs analysis.
- Certified signed indemnity form.
- Specimen signature form.

Once all the above has been assembled it must then be couriered to the bank. Assuming that the account has an associated debit/credit card, then there are two options:

- If you are expected to arrive in the next two weeks then the card will be dispatched to the nearest branch.
- Alternatively, the card can be couriered to you in the UK and you will be required to confirm delivery before the card can be activated.

Once the card is activated it can be used to register for online banking.

7. Foreign Exchange

If you are moving abroad and particularly South Africa, you need to consider foreign exchange (FX) sooner rather than later. Instinctively, many people will turn to their banks as perhaps having dealt with them in the past, they are more comfortable with this option. That's a common mistake people make. Banks tend to charge higher fees and their exchange rates generally aren't all that competitive. In addition, levels of service and the range of products can sometimes be disappointing too. However, as soon as you have made an immigration or removal enquiry, you are likely to be inundated with offers from specialist foreign exchange brokers. Each will claim to offer bank beating rates, probably true, whilst also offering to at least match any other rate offered by the competition.

7.1 FX Brokers

In order to explore these claims, accounts were set-up with three of the major FX brokers, and a number of simulated trades were carried out with different deal sizes on multiple occasions, with the results being averaged. At the same time, we were also fortunate to have a real time data feed showing the mid-market exchange rates. In a perfect world, the trades would be frictionless and the consumer would achieve the mid-market rates. However, in the real world, trades are not frictionless. There are costs associated with commissions, combined with the cost of remitting the bought currency to an overseas account.

The results of our simulated trades are tabulated below and are expressed as a percentage deviation from the mid-market price. In a perfect world a deviation of 0% would be expected but in the real world a smaller negative number in absolute terms would be preferable to a larger value.

Percentage Deviation from Mid-Markets (GBP.ZAR) for Selected Brokers

Deal Size	Percentage Deviation from Mid-Market Rates		
	TorFx[27]	World First[28]	Moneycorp[29]
£1,000	-2.79	-1.85	-3.22
£5,000	-2.85	-1.16	-2.46
£10,000	-2.69	-1.02	-2.28
£25,000	-2.53	-0.94	-2.01
£100,000	NA	-0.87	-1.28

In summary, the results suggest that:

- The exchange rate improves, smaller deviation, as the deal size increases. This should be expected.
- World First remains very competitive across all deal sizes.
- Moneycorp seems to be better suited for larger deals.
- The rates provided by TorFx are relatively insensitive to deal size.

One question that was asked is can I do better than World First? To try and answer that question we looked beyond the specialist currency broker to one of the major on-line brokers, Interactive Brokers (IB). They provide direct access trade execution and clearing services to institutional and professional traders for a wide variety of electronically traded products including stocks, options, futures, forex, bonds, CFDs and funds worldwide. As such, their service is geared towards the professional and frequent trader with no personal service, although they do offer a demo account to let you learn

---

[27] TorFx, see www.torfx.com
[28] World First, see www.worldfirst.com/uk
[29] Moneycorp, see www.moneycorp.com/uk

in a safe environment.

Thus, their service may not be suitable for everyone.

Again, a number of simulated trades were carried out via both IB and World First. In the case of IB, a straightforward comparison using the exchange rate alone is inappropriate, as IB charges commission. Thus, in the table below the IB 'FX Rate' is modified by the commission to give an 'Actual Rate', which can be fairly compared with the World First 'FX rate'. The difference column represents the percentage difference between the World First FX Rate and the IB Actual rate. The results clearly suggest that World First rates can be improved on, particularly for the smaller deal sizes. However, as stated earlier, Interactive Brokers is designed to meet the needs for professional and frequent trades and is not for the faint hearted. In addition, there are restrictions on remitting funds to accounts held in South Africa to anybody other than non-residents.

World First Currency Broker vs. Interactive Stock Broker (IB)

Deal Size	Interactive Brokers[30]			World First	Difference
	FX Rate	Comm	Actual Rate	FX Rate	
£1,000	16.7689	R25.66	16.7432	16.4870	1.55%
£5,000	16.7705	R25.66	16.7654	16.6024	0.98%
£10,000	16.7689	R25.66	16.7663	16.6202	0.88%
£25,000	16.7650	R25.66	16.7640	16.6414	0.74%
£100,000	16.7670	R33.30	16.7667	16.6562	0.66%

---

[30] Interactive Brokers, see www.interactivebrokers.com/en/home.php

7.2 Types of Order

Generally, a broker will offer a number of different order types as summarised below.

Spot Contract

This is probably the most common form of contract for the personal customer in which the contract currencies are exchanged 'on the spot' at the rate quoted, at which point you have entered into a legally binding contract and you will be required to settle the account typically within two working days, after which the bought currency will be remitted to the selected bank account. Unlike banks, the cost of the transfer is normally included in the quoted rate.

Forward Contracts

These are incredibly useful when budgeting for a future currency exchange, as they allow you to fix the rate in advance. For example, if you are building a house and you know that you will need to make a progress payment in three months time, then you can enter into a forward contract and fix the rate today with a settlement date in three months. When you enter into the contract you will be required to make a deposit, typically in the range of 5% (World First) to 10% (TorFx, Moneycorp) with the balance being payable at the agreed settlement date. With a forward contract, this date can be up to two years ahead.

When using a forward contract, there is always the possibility that the broker will issue a margin call requiring the initial deposit to be increased. Such an event, which is uncommon, is however, more likely where only a 5% deposit is specified. The condition when such a margin call can arise is when the exchange rate significantly increases. For example, suppose on the 1st January, R160,000 was purchased at a rate of 16 (ZAR/GBP). Thus, the total cost was £10,000 and a 5% deposit of £500 would be payable. Suppose two months later the exchange rate had improved to 17.0 (ZAR/GBP). If you were unable to complete the transfer the FX broker would be required to sell the R160,000 at a rate of 17.0 which represents a cost of £9,411. This represents a potential loss of £589 (£10,000 - £9,411) which exceeds the initial deposit of £500 and thus a loss to the FX broker. Under such circumstances, you may be asked for an extra top-up to your original deposit, so as to achieve a minimum of a 2% deposit based on the current exchange rate. However, any additional deposit will reduce your final payment and thus you are not paying any more for the currency than originally agreed.

There can be a significant difference between the exchange rate offered by a spot contract and that offered by a forward contract. This is the result of the difference in interest rates between the UK and South Africa. Typically, the interest rate for a saving account in the UK is circa 0.5% whilst it is 7.1% in South Africa, say a difference of 6.6% per annum. Thus, you would expect the forward rate to be circa 6.6% greater than the spot rate based on a one year forward contract. The table below details the forward rates for various forward periods based on a spot rate of 17.8871 GBP.ZAR. The columns 'Percent Change' and 'Annualised Change' refer to the percentage increase above the spot rate.

Forward Contract Pricing

Months Forward	Forward Rate (GBP.ZAR)	Percent Change	Annualised Change
0 (Spot Contract)	17.89 (Spot rate)	0	0
1	17.99	0.56	6.98
2	18.09	1.14	7.04
3	18.18	1.66	6.80
6	18.47	3.28	6.67
12	19.06	6.53	6.53

You will note that the:

- 'Annualised Change' roughly reflects the interest rate difference between the UK and South African savings rate.
- Forward rate is approximately 0.1 (GBP.ZAR) per month greater than the spot rate.
- The advantages of a forward contract are:
- The rate is fixed in advance which allows you to budget.
- Any interest that would be earned is reflected in the contract rate and is therefore not taxable.
- Since you are paying only a small deposit at the time of contract, you can leave the balance invested until the settlement date.

The disadvantage is that the currency won't be available until the agreed settlement date and can't be accessed earlier.

Limit Order

Most of us have other things to do rather than continuously monitor the exchange rate. This is where the limit order comes into play. Using a limit order, you can leave an instruction with your account manager to target a specific exchange rate, which will execute should the rate become available. In practice, such orders are loaded onto their dealing system and thus are monitored 24 hours a day, 5 days a week. An extension to a single limit order is to scale into a position using multiple limit orders.

For example:

- If the GBP.ZAR Spot rate > 17.0 purchase the equivalent of £10K of ZAR
- If the GBP.ZAR Spot rate > 17.1 purchase a further £10K of ZAR etc.

One of the advantages of the limit order is that it takes the emotion out of the trade. On many occasions, we witnessed the spot rate move to a favourable value but then failed to take advantage of the situation because of the mistaken belief/greed that perhaps we could do even better if we delay a bit more, only ultimately to find that the trend has been reversed and we had failed to capitalise on the situation. Hence, the advantage of the limit order is that once you have established the desired target rate, it is entirely mechanical in execution.

Stop Loss Order

If you don't want to trade at the current rate but are concerned that it may worsen and you wish to control the risk, then a stop loss order can be used. This will execute your trade if the exchange rate deteriorates to your specified level. Importantly this allows you to wait for a better rate but also locks in a worst-case rate should the market move against you.

Although we have discussed the various order types individually, it may also be possible, depending on the broker, to combine them. For example, if the spot rate exceeds a particular value then purchase on a forward contract basis.

7.3 Rand Volatility

Historically the Rand has always been a very volatile currency, and it has even been referred to by some as a basket case. A more scientific approach has found that there are three key drivers.

- Global factors in the form of commodity price volatility.
- Economic surprises, with US data being more relevant than South African data.
- Local political uncertainty in terms of both policy and the communication of that policy.

The above will likely come as no surprise to some but the implications are that most of the causes of volatility are outside of South African control. It is assumed that this current trend will persist. Even though we may be unable to predict the volatility, one may still be able to take advantage of it.

The table below details the spot rate for the first trading day for each month for the last fourteen months, together with the minimum ('Min Rate') and maximum ('Max Rate') spot values for the previous 20 trading days. The final column displays the percentage deviation, which is calculated as the difference between the maximum and minimum values divided by the spot value expressed as a percentage. The average monthly deviation is 6.4% and is never less than 3.5%. The implication of this is that by planning ahead we can avoid the need to purchase at a spot rate but can use this volatility to set appropriate limits for either a limit order or to trigger a forward contract and improve the rate achieved.

Monthly Rand Volatility

Date	Spot Rate (GBP.ZAR)	Min Rate	Max Rate	% Dev 20 Days
2-Aug-16	18.68	18.44	19.25	4.37
1-Sep-16	19.50	17.14	19.50	12.12
3-Oct-16	17.53	17.53	19.16	9.27
1-Nov-16	16.59	16.47	17.56	6.56
1-Dec-16	17.73	16.44	17.92	8.39
3-Jan-17	16.89	16.67	17.61	5.54
1-Feb-17	16.98	16.41	17.01	3.51
1-Mar-17	16.05	16.05	16.98	5.76
3-Apr-17	17.10	15.52	17.10	9.25
1-May-17	17.27	16.61	17.27	3.80
1-Jun-17	16.71	16.47	17.63	6.94
4-Jul-17	17.08	16.14	17.08	5.51
1-Aug-17	17.50	16.78	17.50	4.12
1-Sep-17	16.74	16.74	17.52	4.65

7.4 FX Broker Selection

When selecting your FX broker you may wish to consider the following:

- Regulatory compliance.
- Licensed to support you once you have relocated to South Africa.
- Competitiveness of rates including transfer fees across your likely deal sizes.
- Types of order offered.
- Availability and user friendliness of their online trading platform.
- Allocation of a dedicated account manager and general customer service.
- The ability to configure email or SMS alerts based on a target rate being reached.
- Minimum transfer amounts.

Based on both our limited set of simulated trades and our own practical experience over many years, our conditional recommendation for a personal FX broker is World First. Unfortunately, World First is not licensed to deal with 'residents' in South Africa. Their definition of resident is the location where the individual spends the majority of his time. This has nothing to do with tax residence or having the right to reside permanently. Thus, although World First can support you prior to departure, there will come a time when you will need to make alternative arrangements. For those seeking the most competitive deals, then Interactive Brokers should be considered, but as stated earlier, this offering is tailor made for the professional and high frequency trader requiring limit and market orders and is not suitable for everyone.

In conclusion, timing the trade to take advantage of the Rand volatility is more important than FX broker selection.

7.5 Foreign Exchange Controls

South Africa is one of the few countries that continues to operate control over the transfer of money both in and out of the country. This control is affected via the reserve bank, which in turn delegates this to a number of authorised dealers e.g. major retail banks.

In essence:

- There is no issue with bringing money into the country.
- There is no issue in transferring such funds out of the country.
- If the funds are generated internally then there are annual limits on the amount that can leave the country.

You should keep all 'paperwork' associated with the conversion and specifically the transfer of funds into South Africa. Thus, should you ultimately decide to repatriate them, you can clearly demonstrate how and when the funds were introduced.

When transferring funds from the UK it can take up to three working days to be credited to your South African account. As part of this process, you will probably get a phone call from the receiving bank to confirm the purpose of the funds.

8. Rental Accommodation

When looking for rented accommodation there are two major websites:

- Property 24.[31]
- Private Property.[32]

The primary consideration is location and with that, safety and security. Specifically, for South Africa consider:

- Is the property in a gated community (lifestyle or security estate)?
- Secure parking (covered or outside).
- Air conditioning (main bedroom or all bedrooms).
- Heating (open fires are not overly efficient and underfloor electric heating may be too expensive to run).
- Swimming pool or access to a communal pool.

---

[31] Property 24, see ww.property24.com
[31] Private Property, see www.privateproperty.co.za

8.1 The Rental Contract

Typically, property may be rented from any of the major real estate agents and perhaps less commonly, from individuals. However, in all cases, there should be a rental agreement in place. When reviewing the rental contract consider:

- What is the initial lease period?
- After the initial lease does it automatically renew?
- What is the penalty if you break the lease early?
- Is the property up for sale? It is not uncommon for a house to be listed both for sale and for rental. Under such circumstances, what are the arrangements for allowing viewings (number and notice period) and what happens if the accommodation is sold whilst you are the tenant?
- Can you sublet the accommodation? It may be beneficial to find a new tenant for the property rather than break the lease.
- Be aware that in some areas rents may be subject to seasonal variation. A landlord may be comfortable with accepting a longer-term rental in low-season but during high season will want to switch to short term rentals, for which he can charge a premium. As an example, we rented a three bedroom villa in a tourist area for R23,000 per month in low season. In high season the same accommodation is rented out at R4,200 per day!
- There may be an opportunity to negotiate a better rate. In our case, we were able to get a 10% discount in low season just by asking. However, we are not particularly skilled in this area and they agreed to it so readily we thought we should have started at 20%.

8 Rental Accommodation

Ensure the contract clearly identifies who is financially responsible for:

- Refuse?
- Water, some contracts pay for an initial volume per month?
- Electricity?
- Pool services?
- Garden services?
- Alarm maintenance?
- Rates?
- Homeowners' fees or membership fees, only applicable to gated communities?
- DSTV (Sky equivalent) and which packages are included, can you change the package?[33]
- Internet. Clarify whether it is a capped service and what are the likely speeds?

As part of the rental process you will have to:

- Sign the rental agreement and initial every page.
- Provide photocopies of your passport's photo page.
- Provide copy of your right to reside, passport visa or permit.
- Provide Police certificate, which may be required if living in a security or lifestyle estate.

Typically, the contract will require you to pay a one month's rental as a deposit, and sometimes two, together with the first month's rental in advance. Don't be surprised if you are subject to a credit check.

---

[33] DSTV, see www.dstv.com

It is highly recommended that:

- Both you and your spouse sign the rental agreement.
- You get a copy of the agreement once it has been signed by all parties.

The reasoning is that once you get to South Africa you will require proof of address, for example, to get a mobile phone SIM, open a bank account, or get a traffic register number to allow you to purchase a car. A signed rental agreement by all parties meets this requirement.

9. Removals

When deciding which items should be shipped it is worthwhile reviewing the following principles:

- Homes in South Africa are often much larger than the equivalent UK home. Thus, existing UK furniture may be inappropriate.
- Many homes come with fitted bedroom furniture.
- A wide variety of goods is available locally at reasonable prices, so, it may be the case of out with the old and in with the new. For some example prices see Makro's website.[34]
- When shipping goods you are effectively paying for volume, rather than weight, which you are used to when flying. Thus, bulky low-cost items may not be suitable candidates.
- The electrical supply is the same as the UK (230V at 50Hz) and thus your electrical appliances will work. However, the climate in South Africa may mean that the smaller refrigerators that are used in the UK are not appropriate.
- Electrical sockets are known as type M and type N. Type M is a 15 amp plug with 3 round pins which is extensively used. The newer type N socket began to be specified in 2012 and hence is available only in newer houses. One of the benefits of type N is that you no longer need an adaptor for devices that use a double insulated two prong Euro-plug. However, neither socket will accept a UK plug, which is a problem for those portable electronic items that come with a plug with an integrated transformer. Thus, you probably want to remember to bring out your power poles and multi-socket extension leads. It is also probably worth buying a couple of South

---

[34] Makro, see www.makro.co.za

African travel adaptors which can be purchased from some of the eBay vendors.
- In some cases, you may wish to segregate items, as some may be required for immediate delivery e.g. personal electronics, whilst others may require to be stored for a longer term e.g. large items of furniture.
- It is best not to import alcoholic beverages or tobacco products, as these will attract duty and potentially a detailed custom examination.

Having decided what you want to ship then the next question is which removal company are you going to use. When selecting consider the following:

- Does the company specialise in international removals to South Africa? Many domestic removals don't directly handle international moves and will simply sub-contract the work out, which is less than ideal.
- Is the company a member of the British Association of Removals Overseas Group?[35]
- Is the company FIDI Accredited which is an independent quality assurance standard for the international moving industry?[36]
- Check the company's feedback.
- Does it offer a packing service? Don't be tempted to do it yourself. Any savings are likely to be very modest when offset against the increased cost of insurance.
- Does it offer storage at the destination and at what cost?
- Is it asking for a large upfront booking deposit? If so, beware.

---

[35] British Association of Removals Overseas Group, see www.bar.co.uk
[36] FIDI, see www.fidi.org

9.1 Scope of Removals

When comparing costs, the devil is always in the detail, so ensure you understand the scope of supply and the likely costs at all stages. The following headings may prove helpful:

Cost of Packing
- Materials and labour?
- Creating any specialised wooden casing for fragile items such as televisions?
- Have the costs of any disinfecting sprays been included? Typically, outdoor items such as bicycles, garden tools and golf clubs will need to be cleaned in advance of packing and then sprayed.

Transportation
- Transportation to ship.
- Customs clearance, haulage of container and unloading.
- Delivery to the final destination.
- Unpacking and removal of packing materials.
- NES Fee - new export security charge by HMRC.

Insurance Costs
- Rate whilst in transit? Typically, this is based on the declared value, 3% and 3.5%, depending on whether the items have been professionally packed or self-packed respectively.
- Rate whilst in storage, typically 0.3% per month.

It is important to understand whether you have to ensure the entire shipment or whether you can selectively insure individual items. For example, you may decide to insure only those items which by their nature are more prone to damage.

Is it possible/desirable and at what cost to insure against:

- Pairs and sets. If a single item in a set is damaged then it is assumed that the entire set is devalued.
- Mildew. This allows you to claim for damage caused by mildew or mould.
- Electrical/mechanical derangement. This will allow for claims for the malfunction of electrical and mechanical items, even though there is no sign of external damage.

Storage Costs
This are typically quoted on a monthly basis but you can always negotiate for longer periods.

Exclusions
Generally, estimates will also exclude bonding document charges and cargo dues. These are payable by the owner to South African Customs upon arrival.

9.2 Shipping Options

Your removal company may offer you a number of options, depending upon your shipping volume. For example, you may be offered space within a shared container or alternatively you may be offered your own dedicated container. Each option has both pros and cons as summarised below.

Shared Shipping Container
- More economical for smaller volumes.
- Goods are double handled in that they are taken from your premises and then packed into the shared container. Potentially this represents a slightly increased risk of damage and the transit time is likely to be increased (6-10 weeks).

Dedicated Container
- A 20 ft. General purpose container has a volume of 1050 ft^3 and thus this option is going to be viable only if you have more than 700 ft^3 to ship.
- Goods are handled only once so there is a reduced risk of damage and transit times are likely to be reduced (3-5 weeks).
- If you have restricted access it may be impractical to get a dedicated container close to your house.
- The pricing model is slightly more complex, as you will pay one rate for the budgeted volume and volume in excess of this will be charged at a much lower rate.

9.3 Customs Duties

All immigrants and temporary residence visa holders are allowed to import their personal and household effects into South Africa without the payment of import duties and VAT (excluding alcoholic beverages and tobacco products). An inventory of the goods in the container and the visa/permit must be produced to customs. This requires you to be in South Africa at the time your goods arrive.

9.4 Permanent Import of a Car

If you hold a temporary residence visa then the best advice is don't even consider it. Such an import will require:

- Payment of customs duty and VAT. These can easily account for 70% of the market value of the vehicle.
- Import permit (used vehicles only).
- Letter of authority.
- Shipping costs, circa £1,500.

If you hold a permanent residence permit, then it may be viable as you are able to claim the duty back. However, the following conditions must be met:

- You should have owned the vehicle for a period of 12 months prior to your departure date to South Africa. If you have owned it for a lesser period, then the duty rebate will be reduced on a pro-rate basis. Such a vehicle is not considered to be personally owned unless the importer was at all reasonable times personally present at a place where the vehicle was used.
- Vehicles imported in such a manner cannot be disposed of in any way, including lent or given away, within a 20-month period after it has been cleared by customs.

If you still wish to import your vehicle, employ a specialist company with the necessary expertise in South Africa.

9.5 Estimated Removal Costs

The following costs are based on an estimated volume of 720 ft^3, which miraculously 'grew' between the initial and final packaging, in a dedicated container. Collection was Derby with a destination of Paarl, which is about a one hour drive from Cape Town.[37]

Ref.	Description	Cost
1.	Packing and Transportation • 720 ft^3 in a dedicated container • Wooden casing • NES Security fee • Approved disinfect spray • Additional 308 ft3 at preferential rate	£3,049 £75 £45 £25 £354
2.	Insurance in Transit 3% of £20,000	£600
3.	Cargo Dues (payable locally) • Cargo dues • Customs exam • Bonding documentation	£258 £31 £51
	Total:	£4,488

In addition to the above, we also required long-term storage in Cape Town for which a preferential rate was negotiated. The annual costs including insurance were £1,100.

---

[37] The removal costs are dated June 2017 and the services were provided by PSS International Removals, who come highly recommended.

10. Car Hire

Now is probably the time, if you haven't already done so, to create the family Avios account and combine all those points together. Car hire through either Avios or BA directly is reasonably good value. The only downside appears to be that you can't book a rental period which is more than 28 days. If Avios points aren't your thing then car hire using cash is affordable, particularly for the smaller cars, circa £10 per day.

Experience suggests that directly booking through Avis or Hertz, even for extended rental periods, is not particularly beneficial. It appears preferable to use one of these intermediate websites, such as Auto Europe[38]. Let them do the work of trawling through the major suppliers such as Avis, Hertz, Budget and Sixt. Having rented from a number of suppliers, in all cases, we found the cars to be well presented and maintained. When comparing costs always remember to review the deductibles (theft and collision) together with the miscellaneous charges such as an extra driver.

10.1 Excess Car Hire Insurance

All car hire companies will encourage you to take out their optional collision damage waiver (CDW) to cover the deductibles. The deductibles are fairly modest but if you are uncomfortable with them, and wish to protect yourself, then a third-party product will be a more cost effective alternative than that offered by the hire company. For example, iCarHireInsurance will allow you to buy an annual worldwide multi-trip policy for £59.99, which covers you for excesses of up to £6,000 and there are no exclusions around windscreens, tyres and glass etc.[39]

---

[38] Auto Europe, see www.autoeurope.co.uk
[39] iCarHireInsurance, see www.icarhireinsurance.com

10 CAR HIRE

Two particularly useful features are:

- Covers multiple named drivers.
- Covers a maximum rental period of 65 days on any one rental agreement. This allows you to rent a car for two months, then return it and pick up a replacement vehicle.

Generally, our experience in the Western Cape is that the road surfaces are good without the usual UK potholes, and drivers are relatively considerate.

10.2 International Driving Permit (IDP)

An IDP is an official document that effectively validates your UK driving licence in selected foreign countries. It is sometimes called, incorrectly, an International Driving Licence. Is it required? This one probably falls into the category of useful rather than essential. You can certainly hire a car on your UK licence, but it must be the newer photocard type. However, an IDP serves two purposes:

- Should you ever be unfortunate enough to be stopped by the police then they are likely to be more familiar with an IDP rather than a UK licence.
- It can also be used as photo ID. When visiting a security or lifestyle estate you will be asked for photo ID for which you can use your IDP. This avoids the need to carry your passport.

An IDP can be obtained from the RAC[40] for a minimal cost (£8). It comes in two formats IDP 1926 and 1949; with the 1949 format being required for South Africa. You should be aware that an IDP:

- Can be used only with a UK licence, not as a replacement.
- Is valid for only one year.
- Can be issued only within three months of the required date. Experience suggests that it is issued only 5 working days prior to this date.

---

[40] RAC, see www.rac.co.uk/drive/travel/driving-abroad/international-driving-permit

11. Flights and Travel Insurance

11.1 Flights

Using Cape Town as an example, it is well served by flights, with the following airlines offering either a direct or one stop flight:

- British Airways (direct).
- Emirates via Dubai.
- Qatar via Doha.
- Turkish airlines via Istanbul.
- KLM via Amsterdam.
- Air France via Paris.
- Ethiopian airlines via Addis Ababa.
- South African airways via Johannesburg.

Although BA, with its direct flight, may initially be the most attractive, you may find that there is a very significant premium attached to a one-way ticket. Hence, Emirates or Qatar may provide a more economical solution. One cautionary note with Emirates is that they are very strict with their weight allowance. Their standard hold baggage allowance is 30kg per person, which is in-line with all the others. However, we were each two kilos over, which I thought I would get away with. Wrong, we were charged £40 per kilo which I thought was a bit excessive. You can purchase additional weight in advance, but only in 5kg increments, and at a cost that is only discounted by 10%. Don't even think about transferring any excess weight to your hand luggage, as I have seen them weigh that as well. In fairness to Emirates, the weight allowance is well documented so I shouldn't complain.

When going through passport control on arrival, if you have a visa mention it to the border control staff, as they record its details rather than just stamping your passport.

11.2 Travel Insurance

The usual single or multi-trip insurance policies will not suffice, as effectively you are making a one-way trip. It is not clear why they don't, as the policies are generally suitable for a maximum stay of 30 days. Probably just a way of extracting a bit more money from you. However, if you did try and make a claim, they would ask for proof of both your outbound and inbound connection, which could be a bit of a problem.

Thus, if you want to take out travel insurance, you need a specialised policy (one way). One possible supplier is GoWalkAbout.[41]

---

[41] GoWalkAbount, see www.go-walkabout.co.uk

12. Miscellaneous

12.1 Car Navigation System

Before leaving the UK get a TomTom with worldwide maps and lifetime updates. Ensure that South African maps are installed and that they have recently been updated. Thereafter, on landing and picking up the hire car, you are ready to go. Two words of caution. Firstly, postcodes cover a wide area and aren't suitable for navigation, and secondly, there is a tendency of renaming streets. Nevertheless, our TomTom has served us well, with the exception that its POI (Points of Interest) database could be more extensive.

12.2 Winter Temperatures

On reviewing the climate data, you may be expecting mild outside temperatures over winter. Although the statement is true, it does not reflect that temperatures drop significantly at night. Although the winters are relatively mild and short in duration, the houses may be poorly insulated and heated. In our case, we selected a very picturesque villa with stable doors and beautiful high ceilings. Before signing the lease, we confirmed that it had heating. In reality, the house hadn't been lived in for a couple of months prior to our arrival and was freezing. The doors leaked cold air and the only heating was an open fire, supplemented with 400W heating panels which were completely ineffective. Ultimately, we burnt over a thousand logs over a two month period and that only succeeded in keeping the house slightly warmer than outside. Nevertheless, I am sure the birds appreciated it!

12.3 eBook Readers

One of the things we miss is Amazon, and although Kindles are available, they are relatively expensive. We came equipped with a Kindle PaperWhite and an Android tablet. However, the intensity of the sunlight means that the tablet is ineffective as a reader. So, if you are keen readers, come prepared.

Part 3: On Arrival

13. Telecommunications

13.1 Mobile Phones

A mobile phone is essential in South Africa and is extensively used by the banks as part of the authentication process when using on-line banking. The four major network providers are:

Mobile Operator	Subscribers (K)	Market Share (%)
Vodacom[42]	37,100	42.1
MTN[43]	30,800	34.9
Cell C[44]	15,000	17.3
Telekom[45]	3,999	4.5
Others	1,000	1.1

Vodacom is the most dominant provider. Cell C is one of the fastest growing providers and has the lowest percentage of customer complaints, whilst Telkom and MTN are struggling with customer loyalty. However, South Africa is vast and perhaps the key selection criterion is the quality of coverage in your area.

Once the provider has been selected, you can simply visit one of the cellular stores that proliferate the larger shopping malls. You will need your passport and signed rental agreement, as proof of address, and that will enable you to purchase a SIM for R1 and charge it with an appropriate quantity of air-time.

Thereafter, you can re-charge your phone either by visiting one of the many stores or directly via your local bank account either by an ATM or on-line banking.

---

[42] Vodacom, see www.vodacom.co.za
[43] MTN, see www.brightside.mtn.co.za
[44] Cell C, see www.cellc.co.za/cellc/home
[45] Telekom, see www.telkom.co.za/today

13.2 VOIP Phones

If you had elected to take out a local VOIP phone number before arriving in South Africa you would have been given a non-geographical number, typically starting with 087. Once you have signed a rental agreement you can use this as the basis to request a geographical number. Such numbers cover very large areas. For example, the Western Cape covers an area of 129,462 km^2 and yet has only six area codes allocated to it. Thus, once you have your local VOIP number you can likely take it with you as you move.

14. Tax

This section has been written after careful research. Nevertheless, like many economies, there is a tendency for government to tinker continually with the tax legislation so as to maximise their revenue stream. Therefore, the information provided is not a substitute for advice from a professional who can consider your personal circumstances.

Benjamin Franklin famously said, 'there are only two things certain in life: death and taxes'. If we limit our discussions to income tax, then emigrating to South Africa may disprove this one aspect of the quote. The key question to ask in this respect is where am I tax resident, UK or South Africa? In extreme cases, you could be tax resident in both countries. Fortunately, many countries, including the United Kingdom and the Republic of South Africa, have double taxation agreements, which usually provide rules to determine which of the two countries will treat you as a tax resident.

14.1 Am I Tax Resident in South Africa?

This is a slightly easier question to ask as the rules are somewhat simpler. The tax year in South Africa runs from the 1st of March to the last day in February. To be a tax resident you must meet the requirements of either being an 'ordinary resident' or the 'physical presence test'.

14 TAX

Ordinarily Resident

An individual will be considered to be ordinarily resident in South Africa if it is the country to which that individual will naturally, and as a matter of course, return after his or her wanderings. It could be described as that individual's usual or principal residence, or his or her real home. Thus, the following two requirements must be met:

- An intention to become ordinarily resident in a country; and
- Steps indicative of this intention have been or are being carried out.

Hence, for example, if an application was made for permanent residency or a house was purchased as a primary residence, then this could be interpreted as meeting the requirements of being an ordinary resident.

Physical Presence Test

Under the physical presence test the individual must meet all of the following three requirements regarding their presence in South Africa, which must exceed:

- 91 days in total during the year of assessment under consideration; and
- 91 days in total during each of the five years of assessment preceding the year of assessment under consideration; and
- 915 days in total during those five preceding years of assessment.

If you are not ordinarily resident, nor meet the requirements of the physical presence test, then you will be regarded as a non-resident for tax purposes. This means that you will be subject to tax only on income that has its source in South Africa, for example, interest earned from a South African Bank; rental income earned from a property in South Africa; and services rendered in South Africa.

14.2 Am I Tax Resident in the UK?

Surely if I am not tax resident in South Africa, then I must be tax resident in the UK? Not true. The UK applies its own test for residence known as the Statutory Residence Test[46]. This consists of three groups of questions. The first group of questions is used to determine if you are automatically classified as a non-resident as shown below. If you are classified as non-resident, then there is no need to progress to the second and third group of questions.

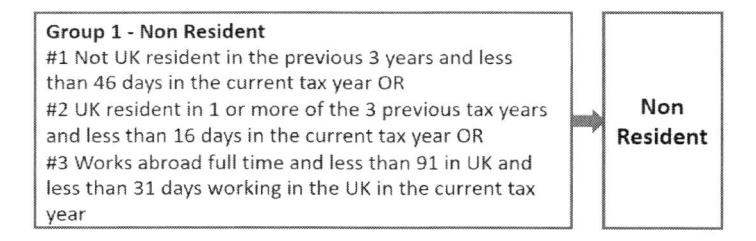

Group 1 - Non Resident
#1 Not UK resident in the previous 3 years and less than 46 days in the current tax year OR
#2 UK resident in 1 or more of the 3 previous tax years and less than 16 days in the current tax year OR
#3 Works abroad full time and less than 91 in UK and less than 31 days working in the UK in the current tax year

➡ **Non Resident**

If the first group is inconclusive then you should proceed to the second group to determine if you are automatically classified as a resident. You would only proceed to the third group if the results are still inconclusive.

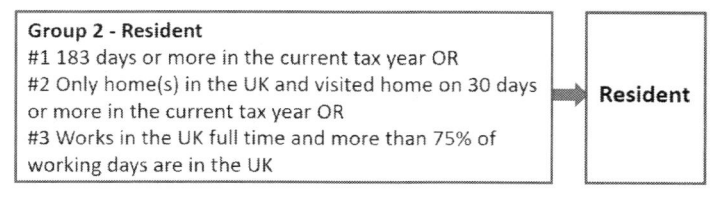

Group 2 - Resident
#1 183 days or more in the current tax year OR
#2 Only home(s) in the UK and visited home on 30 days or more in the current tax year OR
#3 Works in the UK full time and more than 75% of working days are in the UK

➡ **Resident**

---

[46] For a comprehensive description see:
https://www.gov.uk/government/publications/rdr3-statutory-residence-test-srt

14 TAX

If the output from both the previous groups of questions is inconclusive, then you need to proceed to the final group which is used to measure the number of ties you have with the UK. For each true statement, you score one tie. Hence you have a potential score of 5.

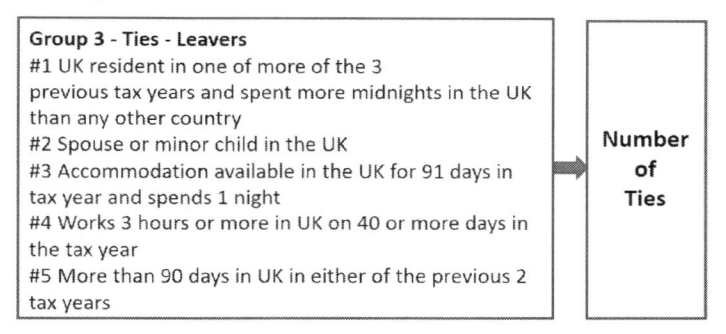

Group 3 - Ties - Leavers
#1 UK resident in one of more of the 3 previous tax years and spent more midnights in the UK than any other country
#2 Spouse or minor child in the UK
#3 Accommodation available in the UK for 91 days in tax year and spends 1 night
#4 Works 3 hours or more in UK on 40 or more days in the tax year
#5 More than 90 days in UK in either of the previous 2 tax years

➡ **Number of Ties**

Finally, using the table below, and based on the number of ties combined with the time spent in the UK will determine whether you are a resident or non-resident for tax purposes.

Ref	Days in UK Current Tax Year	Status
1.	0 - 15	Not Resident
2.	16 - 45	Resident if 4 or more ties
3.	46 - 90	Resident if 3 or more ties
4.	91 - 120	Resident if 2 or more ties
5.	121 - 182	Resident if 1 or more ties
6.	183 or more	Resident

Examples

Let us suppose you have left the UK in September. If you apply the Statutory Residence Test (SRT) you would find that the first group of questions is inconclusive and therefore you move on to the second group. However, when you evaluate question 2 concerning homes you will probably find that you are UK tax resident and thus there is no need to progress to the third group.

It is now April 5th, new UK tax year, and you have been in South Africa since September. You apply the SRT a second time. This time questions in groups one and two are inconclusive, so you progress to the third group. In this third group, two of the questions, #1 and #5 are probably true and therefore you have two ties. From the above table, you can see that if you have two ties and have spent less than 91 days in the UK in the current tax year then you are classified as non-resident.

14.3 Why is this Important?

According to section 10(1)(gC) of the South African Tax Laws, the following will be exempt from normal tax:

- Amount received by or accrued to any resident under the social security system of any other country or
- Lump sum, pension or annuity received by or accrued to any resident from a source outside the Republic as consideration for past employment outside the Republic other than from any pension fund, pension preservation fund, provident fund, provident preservation fund or retirement annuity fund as defined in section 1(1) excluding any amount transferred to that fund from a source outside the Republic in respect of that member.

14 TAX

In summary, subject to you being classified as a non-UK tax resident, then any income derived from a foreign source, assuming it is not associated with activities carried out in South Africa, is exempt from income tax.

However, although the pension is tax exempt, you must declare all foreign pensions. The South African Revenue Service (SARS) will require supporting evidence and therefore you should bring any documentation relating to your pension plans.

14.4 Other Sources of Income

Income Tax

Although foreign pensions are tax exempt, other sources are taxed using a progressive tax system. Tax thresholds for individual income tax are:

Ref.	Person	2018 Threshold
1.	Under 65	R75,750 (£4,509)
2.	65 and older	R117,300 (£6,982)
3.	75 and older	£131,150 (£7,806)

Rates of tax for individuals are:

Ref.	Taxable Income (R)	2018 Tax Rates
1.	R0 – R189,880 (£0 – R11,302)	18% of taxable income
2.	R189,881 – R296,540 (£11,302 – £17,651)	R34,178 (£2,034) + 26% of taxable income above R189,880 (£11,302)
3.	R296,541 – R410,460 (£17,651 – £24,432)	R61,910 (£3,685) + 31% of taxable income above R296,540 (£17,651)
4.	R410,461 – R555,600 (£24,432 – £33,071)	R97,225 (£5,787) + 36% of taxable income above R410,460 (£24,432)
5.	R555,601 – R708,310 (£33,071 – £42,161)	R149,475 (£8,897) + 39% of taxable income above R555,600 (£33,071)
6.	R708,311 – R1,500,000 (£42,161 – £89,286)	R209,032 (£12,442) + 41% of taxable income above R708,310 (£42,161)

There is little opportunity for a retired person to reduce his income tax payable in South Africa. However, one area is the Medical Scheme Fees Tax Credit (MTC). This is a rebate which reduces the normal tax a person pays. It is non-refundable and any portion that is not allowed in the current year cannot be carried over to the next year of assessment.

For 2018 it is:

- R303 (£18.4) per month for the taxpayer who paid the medical scheme contributions.
- R303 (£18.4) per month for the first dependant.

14 Tax

Interest

Interest from a South African source earned by a natural person is exempt, per annum, up to an amount of:

Ref.	Person	2018 Threshold
1.	Under 65	R23,800 (£1,417)
2.	65 and older	R34,500 (£2,053)

A final withholding tax of 15% will be charged on interest payable to non-residents. However, there are a number of exceptions. The result of these is that the interest is likely to be paid gross but you are still responsible for paying any tax liability arising where you are tax resident.

For residents, any interest above the threshold would potentially attract income tax. However, any such interest, above the threshold, would be appended to any other taxable income. This total income would then be tested against the income tax threshold to determine if any tax is payable. Thus, suppose you are under 65 and have accumulated interest on your savings account of R90,000 but have no other taxable income. Under such circumstances, you would be entitled to subtract your interest exemption of R23,800 and your income tax exemption of R75,750. Since these exemptions exceed the earned interest, then no tax liability would arise.

Tax on Shares

Non-residents are generally subject to only CGT (Capital Gains Tax) on the disposal of shares in companies holding immovable property in South Africa. However, as a resident, you will be taxed on either an income or CGT basis, depending upon the objective of holding the shares.

Shares held as trading stock are ones that you bought for the main purpose of reselling at a profit. Any gain or loss you make on the disposal of a share you held as a trading stock will be taxed on an income basis. As such you will be taxed at your marginal rate.

By contrast, if you hold a share as a capital asset (that is, as a long-term dividend-producing investment) any gain or loss upon its disposal will be of a capital nature.

Thus, if you have an equity portfolio it may be beneficial, if possible, to hold them within a UK SIPP (Self Invested Personal pension) and thereby avoid any tax liability. If you have a SIPP, and even if you have no relevant UK earnings, you can still continue to contribute to it. No tax relief is available on the additional contributions, nor are there any restrictions on the amount. However, you would wish to ensure you don't exceed the lifetime allowance, which is currently £1M for 2017/18.

14.5 Capital Gains Tax (CGT)

Primary Residence
Unlike the UK, the sale of your primary residence may be subjected to capital gains. However, in most cases it will not be applicable as the first R2M of any capital gain or loss on the sale is disregarded for CGT purposes. Assuming the house is held in joint names, then effectively you have an allowance of R4M. Although this allowance is not automatically indexed, in practice, it has periodically been increased, for example:

- 1st March 2006: R1M
- 1st March 2012: R1.5M

When calculating capital gains, you can include the cost of any improvements, but not routine maintenance, within the base price.

14 TAX

Other Capital Gains

Capital gains may be applicable to other assets, such as the sale of shares. For these other assets the annual exemption is as follows:

Ref.	Person	2018 Threshold
1.	Natural Person	R40,000 (£2,380)
2.	Natural person - in year of death	R300,000 (£17,857)

The capital gains rate for individuals, above the thresholds, for 2018 is 18%.

14.6 Inheritance Tax (Estate Tax)

In South Africa, estate duty is not payable on any asset bequeathed to a spouse[47]. However, estate duty is payable on the estate of every person who dies and whose net estate is in excess of R3.5M. It is charged at the rate of 20%. In the case of a surviving spouse, the R3.5M from the predeceased's estate may be used to provide a total exemption of R7M.

---

[47] Wealth warning. The Davis Tax Committee has made recommendations on estate duty and donations tax which, if adopted, would have a significant impact on estate duty when an asset is left to the surviving spouse. Further information is unlikely to be available until February 2018.

14.7 Other Tax Questions

Should you still have outstanding questions concerning taxation then two possible options are recommended:

- SARS (South African Revenue) operate a site known as TaxTim. You can register free of charge and ask basic tax questions. Typically, they will respond within two working days. Should the questions become more complex, they will ask for payment, circa R399 (£23.75).[48]
- South African Tax Guide[49] contains a wealth of information on tax matters and is run by an accountant, Nyasha Musviba[50]. For a small fee, he can assist with anything from providing comprehensive and understandable answers to simple tax questions through to assisting with estate planning.

---

[48] TaxTim, see www.taxtim.com/za/get-started
[49] South African Tax Guide, see www.sataxguide.co.za
[50] Nyasha is based in Cape Town and can be contacted by email (nyasha@sataxguide.co.za) or telephone (084 969 0510)

15. UK Pensions

15.1 Private Pension

If you are no longer tax resident in the UK you may think that you can no longer contribute to a UK pension and get tax relief, a reasonable assumption but an incorrect one.

An individual may be a member of a UK registered scheme, regardless of nationality or residence, however, tax relief on personal contributions will depend on which of the following categories apply:

- Individuals with earnings chargeable to UK tax, or who are UK resident, are able to get tax relief on contributions up to £3,600 or 100% of earnings if greater but subject to the maximum annual allowance.
- Non-resident individuals who do not have UK earnings will get no tax relief on personal contributions.
- Non-resident individuals who do not have UK earnings, but who were included within the first bullet point within the last 5 years and were UK resident when he/she joined the pension scheme will get tax relief on contributions up to £3,600.

So, in essence, according to the last bullet point you can continue to contribute £2,880 annually into your existing pension plan, which will be increased to £3,600 with tax relief, for 5 years even though you are not UK tax resident.

In addition to the above, you can continue to contribute to your private pension, without limits, although you will not get any tax relief. This may be useful as it allows you to transfer assets in the form of cash, for example, sell shares held outside a pension plan, and invest the proceeds into your plan. Thus, they will be protected by the pension wrapper as, if you are tax resident in South Africa, all income from foreign pensions is exempt from income tax. Such gross contributions may not be supported by all SIPP administrators.

15.2 State Pension

With the introduction of the new state pension, you will need 35 qualifying years to get a full pension. Alternatively, you will need a minimum of 10 qualifying years to get any pension. The problem here is 'qualifying' years, as some employees who were 'contracted out' of the state pension paid lower NI contributions and may, therefore, be eligible for less than the full new state pension, even if they have worked for 35 years. You are most likely to be impacted if you have been a member of a defined benefits (final salary) pension scheme, for example, teachers, nurses, civil servants and local government workers.

For most people, the most cost effective method of adding qualifying years is to make class 3 voluntary contributions. For example, a single year of contributions can be bought for a lump sum of around £741. This will boost your state pension entitlement by around £237 a year for the rest of your life. Hence, the single contribution of £741 would equate to an additional £4,740 over the course of a 20-year retirement, which is a very useful return on your initial investment.[51]

However, too much of a good thing can also be bad for your financial health, as there is nothing to be gained by having more than 35 qualifying years.

---

[51] For more information see: https://www.gov.uk/voluntary-national-insurance-contributions

16. Health Care

16.1 General Practitioners

Assuming you have your medical aid or equivalent in place then there is probably little to do. However, if you have a chronic condition then you will probably want to 'register' with a GP, generally known as FP (Family Practitioners in South Africa) so that he can examine you and write the necessary repeat prescription. Assuming you have medical aid, then the scheme may cover you immediately depending upon the exclusions they imposed when the plan was first taken out. Regardless, it is still probably worthwhile using one of their network FPs to ensure continuity of care. From your schemes website, you can get a list of providers. In many cases, you may find that healthcare professionals have amalgamated to create a medical centre. One such group is Medicross. For example, at our local Medicross centre there are probably six FPs, together with dentists, opticians, dietitians, physios, a pathology and an ultrasound department. These facilities are normally centrally located with plenty of parking. Thus, you can have a single centre for the majority of your healthcare needs.[52]

FPs appear to do more than perhaps their UK equivalents. As an example, I visited one to get a prescription for my chronic medication. Frankly, I expected a 15 minute appointment and a superficial examination. How wrong I was after emerging an hour later having had:

- Full physical examination.
- Resting and exercise ECG.
- A full set of blood tests.

Approximately two days later the FP phoned me at home to explain all the blood results.

---

[52] Medicross, see http://www.medicross.co.za

16.2 Prescriptions and Chronic Medication

An FP by law can write a prescription for only six months of medication. However, such medication can only be called off from the pharmacist on a monthly basis. If you have a chronic condition that is covered by your medical aid, then the condition must be registered with them, together with the proposed drug therapy. This is largely done by your FP. Assuming that this is approved by your medical aid, then you should be able to take your prescription to their designated pharmacist, who will then fill it without charge. It is important to use the designated pharmacist or you may be subject to a co-payment. It is possible that the medical aid scheme may accept the diagnosis but reject the medication as it is not on their approved list for your condition. Under such circumstances there are two options:

- Pay for the medication personally.
- Challenge the rejection either directly yourselves or through your FP. Even if successful you may still have to make a co-payment to cover the drug.

16.3 Pharmacist Services

The larger pharmacy groups will typically provide a number of health services, often a more comprehensive offering than that found in the UK. This can extend from basic wound care through to screening and vaccinations. Some examples of costs are shown in appendix 4.

17. Buying a Car

Before you can buy a car in South Africa you will need a traffic register number.

17.1 Traffic Register Number

South African residents are automatically loaded on to the National Transport Information System (eNaTIS). This system is the national register that stores, records, manages and enforces the requirements of the National Road Traffic Act (NRTA) and the National Road Traffic Regulations (NRTR).

To register a car in your name in South Africa you need to be loaded on the eNaTIS system, and as such, foreigners need first to apply for a Traffic Register Number (ANR). This number is the main identification accepted for road traffic transactions on the eNaTIS system for foreigners.

To apply for a Traffic Register Number, you will need to visit your nearest Registering Authority or Licensing Centre and complete the application form. Specifically, you will need the following:

- Copy of your passport picture page.
- Copy of your residency visa/permit.
- Two passport photographs.
- Proof of address as detailed below.

For this any one of the following is acceptable:

- Utility account (water, electricity, sewerage or refuse collection).
- Bank statement.
- Municipal rates and taxes invoice.
- Telephone account.
- Official letter from the South African Revenue Service.
- Correspondence from a Corporate body.
- Retail store statement.
- Letter from the administration department for applicants living in any type of residence.
- Letter with an official date stamp from an educational institution.

All of the above must not be more than three months old.

An alternative is a mortgage statement which is not more than six months old.

The other possibilities, providing they are not older than one year are:

- A lease agreement signed by all parties.
- An official tax return/tax assessment.
- Valid television license.
- Insurance policy document.

The application form is known as ANR (Application and Notice in respect of traffic register number).[53]

---

[53] The ANR form may be downloaded from:
www.enatis.com/index.php/downloads/cat_view/12-public/4-forms/8-road-traffic-related-forms?limit=5&order=name&dir=ASC&start=10

The form is submitted with the associated documentation at the local licensing centre and you should be contacted within six weeks to collect your register number.

You can expect some regional variation to the above procedure but general points to note are:

- If you want to register the vehicle in both names then you must apply for two register numbers.
- You must ensure that the form is submitted in the municipal area in which you reside.
- Others have reported that the copies of the passport and visa have to be certified, although this was not our experience. This can be done free of charge at the local police station.

17.2 Vehicle Registration

A vehicle needs to be registered on change of ownership. This typically costs R150 (£8.93).

17.3 Annual Licence Fee

The annual licence fee depends on the province, category of vehicle, and its tare weight. However, examples for the Western Cape are:

Ref	Category	Tare Weight (kg)	Annual Cost
1.	Motor Cycle	NA	R168 (£10)
2.	Car	1001-1250	R393 (£23.39)
3.	Car	1251-1500	R537 (£31.96)
4.	Car	1501-1750	R592 (£35.24)

17.4 Annual Vehicle Inspection

There are approximately 12M vehicles registered in South Africa. For 80% of the vehicles on the roads, roadworthy testing is only required on change of ownership. Vehicles operated for reward, heavy goods vehicles as well as taxis, are required to be tested annually, whilst buses are required to be tested every 6 months.

The current roadworthy legislation requires a roadworthy certification under the following circumstances:

- A used vehicle of which the owner has changed.
- A motor vehicle to which a notice to discontinue has been issued.
- A motor vehicle built, imported, or manufactured.
- A reconstructed or altered motor vehicle.
- Taxis and trucks weighing more than 3500kg.
- Buses tested every 6 months.

The Minister of Transport has published legislation for the future that will entail all vehicles, 10 years and older, to undertake a road worthiness test every 2 years. Currently, there is no date set for implementation.

17.5 Insurance

Approximately 70% of all registered vehicles are uninsured. However, in South Africa all drivers have limited protection via the Road Accident Fund (RAF)[54]. This fund exists to cover for loss or damage resulting from death or bodily injury caused by the negligent driving of motor vehicles within South Africa. The fund itself is substantially funded by a levy on petrol and diesel fuel. From the fund you can claim for:

- Past and future hospital and medical expenses.
- Past and future loss of income or earnings.
- Past and future loss of support for a dependent of a deceased victim.
- General damages for pain, suffering and disfigurement in the case of bodily injury.
- However, the fund does not cover damage to any property.

For more comprehensive cover you will need specifically to take out insurance. This can be relatively expensive due to both car theft and the high cost of imported components required for repairs. SUV's and bakkies are particularly desirable, as they can be readily sold to neighbouring countries. As you would expect, insurance costs are also very dependent on the province[55], with the Western Cape accounting for only 7% of all vehicle hijacking and theft. Examples of monthly insurance costs for various vehicles are detailed in the table below.

---

[54] Road Accident Fund (RAF), see www.raf.co.za
[55] See www.arrivealive.co.za/Hijackings-Where-When-and-Which-Vehicles

In all cases:

- Vehicle is a 2017 model located in an access controlled area in Paarl (Western Cape). This area has a relatively low incidence of car hijacking/theft.
- Driver is a 58 year old male, with 7 years of no claims, driving under an International licence.

Example Insurance Costs

Ref	Car	Type of Insurance	Monthly Cost
1.	Mazda 2	Comprehensive	R630 (£37.50)
2.	Mazda 2	Third Party + Fire and Theft	R277 (£16.49)
3.	Mazda MX5	Comprehensive	R883 (£52.56)
4.	Mazda MX5	Third Party + Fire and Theft	R296 (£17.62)
5.	BMW 1 Series 118	Comprehensive	R939 (£55.89)
6.	BMW 1 Series 118	Third Party + Fire and Theft	R291 (£17.32)

There appears to be a slight increase in cost if driven under a South African licence.

17.6 Cost of Purchasing a Car

Car prices in South Africa are generally seen as expensive, particularly when compared with salaries. The following table compares the cost of new cars in both South Africa and the UK. The smaller cars are slightly less expensive than the equivalent UK vehicle, but as you move up through the price range, the price gap widens. Options to lease rather than buy a vehicle outright are limited.

Car Purchase Costs UK vs. South Africa

Ref	Car	Cost UK	Cost South Africa	Percent Difference
1.	Mazda 2	£13,695	R215,100 (£12,803)	-6.5%
2.	Mazda MX5	£27,965	R532,800 (£31,714)	13.4%
3.	BMW 1 Series 118	£21,430	R417,942 (£24,877)	16.0%
4.	Mercedes SLC	£32,439	R714,600 (£42,535)	31.1%

Previously owned car prices are also high. A consequence of this is that the depreciation rates are lower than the UK, particularly for the smaller cars. Both the Auto trader[56] and Cars[57] websites can be useful for price comparison purposes.

If purchasing a new car, the following accessories should be considered:

- Paint protection - An additional lacquer to help protect the paintwork from discolouration due to the strong sunlight.
- Window safety film, sometimes known as smash and grab - Offers UV resistance and limits forced entry into your vehicle.
- Auto-locking - Central locking is activated when the car starts or reaches a particular speed.

---

[56] Auto trader, see www.autotrader.co.za
[57] Cars, see www.cars.co.za

18. Buying Property

18.1 Property Price Trends

All too often I hear from seasoned estate agents that house prices are rising rapidly, in an attempt to create the illusion that there is urgency in the decision process, and that you must act now to avoid disappointment. Research may back this up, as published statements based on the FNB (First National Bank) property price index on a year on year basis (circa June 2016 - June 2017) suggest that prices in Euro, USD and GBP terms have risen by 24.3%, 19.3% and 36.5% respectively.[58]

However, these eye watering figures concerning the state of the real estate market don't seem to agree with our observations. As is frequently the case, the devil is in the detail. For the period from 1st June 2016 to 1st June 2017, the Rand appreciated by 19.7%, 20.0% and 34% against the Euro, USD and GBP respectively. Thus, much of the increase in house prices is down to currency appreciation rather than the asset itself.

Hence, what is really happening to house prices? Lightstone[59] Property provides a view on the property market both on a residential and commercial basis.

---

[58] See Foreigner's guide to buying property in South Africa (www.property24.com/articles/foreigners-guide-to-buying-property-in-south-africa/25941)
[59] Lightstone property, see www.lightstoneproperty.co.za

18 Buying Property

Based on their data, the graph below shows annual price increases for residential property over the last four years[60]. What we do see is that the lower value banded property is appreciating strongly, whilst the middle and high value bands are appreciating much more modestly at around 5% per annum. For the luxury segment, we can see that price increases are much more subdued at around 1% per annum. If you looked at the monthly luxury data for July and August 2017 you would note price deflation.

Property band value is defined as follows:

Ref	Property Band	Value (R)
1.	Luxury	> R1.5M
2.	High	R700K to R1.5M
3.	Mid	R250K to R700K
4.	Low	<R250K

---

[60] For 2017 it is based on an average value calculated from the first 8 months only.

What happens to property prices if you factor in inflation? If you adjusted price inflation by the consumer price index[61] then you would find that, excluding low value property, prices for the middle and high value properties are stagnant in real terms, with the luxury properties contracting at about 4% per year.

Real Terms Annual Price Increase vs. Property Value Band (Adjusted against CPI)

However, the above are very broad trends across South Africa. If you break down the data on an individual province basis, as shown in the table below, you will see that both the Northern and Western Cape are experiencing much higher house inflation.

---

[61] CPI data is available from Statistics South Africa (www.statssa.gov.za)

Annual Price Increase (%) vs. Province

Ref	Province	2013	2014	2015	2016	2017	Avg
1.	Eastern Cape	3.4	4.0	3.5	5.0	5.2	4.2
2.	Free State	3.9	5.6	2.7	4.8	4.2	4.2
3.	Gauteng	5.1	5.2	4.0	3.4	3.3	4.2
4.	Kwazulu Natal	4.5	5.3	5.2	5.3	4.5	5.0
5.	Western Cape	6.5	7.9	9.2	8.5	8.3	8.1
6.	Northern Cape	17.3	14.1	13.4	16.3	19.4	16.1
7.	North West	6.0	3.4	2.4	1.1	2.4	3.1
8.	Mpumalanga	7.8	2.8	3.3	2.1	2.0	3.6
9.	Limpopo	5.5	6.8	5.2	3.4	6.8	5.5

18.2 Gated vs. Residential Area Living

Having decided upon the general area, the next decision is do you want to live within a gated community or just in a village or town? Not an easy choice.

Gated Community

In its simplest form, a gated community may be nothing more than a collection of a dozen houses or so with some fencing around them, combined with some form of access control, which could be nothing more than a set of automated gates. This can probably be described as a security estate, as its primary function is to control access. At the other end of the spectrum, you will find lifestyle estates such as Pearl Valley[62] and Val de Vie[63].

---

[62] Pearl Valley, see www.pearlvalley.co.za
[63] Val de Vie, see www.valdevie.co.za

Typically, these will be built around a theme such as golf, polo etc. and in addition, offer extensive communal facilities such as a gymnasium, tennis and squash courts, swimming pool, walking trails and gardens.

Our first visit to a lifestyle estate was in 2016 when we were scheduled to visit Pearl Valley, which is one of the more secure estates, to look at some property. This is the same estate where the retired English cricketer Geoffrey Boycott has his winter home. At the time I was not a great believer in security estates and had explained to my wife that if I see a single person with a gun then I know the place is not for me. With some trepidation I drove up to the security gate to book in, fully expecting to be greeted by a massive ex-military security guard armed to the teeth with automatic weapons. The guard turned out to be a young lady who wouldn't look out of place as a hotel receptionist, armed with a welcoming smile. With relief, I had to agree that the first test was passed. Whilst I was waiting for her to confirm my appointment with the host, I eagerly started a conversation around her exciting life, and whether she ever had to deal with any thieves breaching the perimeter fencing. Much to my surprise, she said there had been an incident some two months before. My ears pricked up, tell me more. Ultimately it was an anti-climax as the potential thief ended up being a baby leopard trying to dig under the fence.

Although gated communities can be attractive to some, they also come with a number of disadvantages:

- All the supporting infrastructure, whether it is just security or a golf course, comes at a cost. Such costs are passed onto the owners as levies and typically can cost each owner R4,000 (£238.10) per month, which is in addition to property rates.
- Homeowners have to abide by the Home Owners Association (HOA) rules and regulations. These can include anything from the booking in procedure for visitors, road speed limits, landscaping standards, colours that can be used when painting the external walls of your home, pets and property letting. Some people may find the rules overbearing and incompatible with their lifestyle.
- Although the smaller gated communities may be wholly contained within the town, some of the larger ones, simply because of the area they occupy, are more remote and require a car to access facilities in the local town. Under these circumstances, you can't just amble down to your local coffee shop or restaurant and thus you may feel slightly detached from the local community. This may be offset, as there is some anecdotal evidence that people within a gated environment are more likely to connect, and thus act to ensure that everyone is content.

Residential Area Living
The vast majority of people, some 95%, live outside a gated community. They perhaps don't have the benefits of some of the shared resources available within a gated environment but then they aren't paying for them either. It all comes down to personal choice. There is a tendency for the better homes to be located within a gated area. For example, although such homes account for only 5% of the housing stock in numeric terms, it is 15% when measured in terms of market value.

18.3 Property Options
When purchasing property, the vast majority of people will opt to purchase property either directly from a developer as a new build, or more likely as a resell. However, these are not the only options. For the more adventurous of you, there is the possibility of either adopting a 'Plot and Plan' approach or a complete custom design.

Plot and Plan Approach
This option is particularly prevalent within the gated communities where a developer will offer a plot together with a number of 'standard' designs with a series of options. Such options may include a: swimming pool, PV solar array, jacuzzi or fire pit, as well as your choice for a range of standard surface finishes. These are often very attractively priced, and within the costs, there is normally an allowance of 10-15 hours of architectural design to make minor changes. In our particular case, when we investigated further, it became clear that the developer wanted us to place the total cost of the build in an escrow account at the start of the contract, which would then be administered by a conveyancing agent. The agent would then pay the developer against signed progress certificates, which would be issued by an independent party. For the duration of the build, the interest that accrued within the account would be credited to the purchaser's account. In effect, you have lost all control over the funds for the duration

of the build which we were uncomfortable with. In the defence of this option, these estates have a reputation to maintain. The developers have previously been screened and only accredited companies are allowed to offer this option You should expect to be able to view examples of their work, but perhaps not necessarily your particular 'standard' design. The devil is always in the detail, so ensure you understand what standard of finishes are included in the base price.

Based on the Val De Vie estate which is South African's premier lifestyle estate some example prices for a plot and plan would be:[64]

Example Plot and Plan Prices

Ref	Property Description	Area Living Area & Plot Size	Price	Price Per M² Living Area
1.	3 beds, 2 baths, 1 garage	177 M² 424 M²	R3,977K £237K	R22.5K £1.34K
2.	4 beds, 3 baths, 2 garages	226 M² 424 M²	R4,538K £270K	R20.1K £1.19K
3.	4 beds, 3 baths, 2 garages	303 M² 499 M²	R6,304 £375K	R20.8K £1.24K

Living areas in South African houses include all covered areas such as garages and patio. How does this compare to the UK? The table below details sizes and prices for the average UK house.[65]

---

[64] Based on the Le Domaine Vines development. Further information may be found at: https://www.property24.com/new-developments/val-de-vie-estate/val-de-vie/western-cape/le-domaine-vines/11726/1423
[65] Information available from Zoopla, see https://www.zoopla.co.uk/market/uk

Average UK House Sizes and Price

Ref	Property Description	Area (M²) Living Area	Price	Price Per M² Living Area
1.	Detached	115.5 M²	£442K	£3.83K
2.	Semi-Detached	37.4 M²	£271K	£7.25K
3.	Terraced	40.6 M²	£251K	£6.18K

From this, combined with the results from the previous table, we can conclude that houses in South Africa are generally larger than the UK equivalents and that their price per unit area is significantly less.

Custom Design

For those that want a truly unique design, then there is the possibility of purchasing a plot of land, engaging an architect and having the house built. Assuming a reasonably high level of finishes, then the estimated costs for a 440 M² single storey house, excluding land purchase, would be:

18 BUYING PROPERTY

Example Build Costs for the Western Cape

Ref	Description	Cost[66]
1.	Architect Fees	R694K
2.	Other Professional Fees • Structural engineering • Planning fees • Land survey • Geotechnical survey • Health and Safety • Rational design • Kitchen equipment allowance	R210K
3.	Construction Costs • 440 M² Undercover • 30 M² Pergolas	R7,040K R111K
	Total:	**R8,055** **£480K**

In addition to the above, there is also the cost of the plot. Such a house would require a plot of at least 700 M² at a cost of R3K per M². This equates to a total plot cost R2,100K (£125K). Thus, the entire cost would be circa R10,155K (£605K), hardly insignificant, but compared to the 'average' UK detached house, it is almost four times larger but is almost 40% more expensive.

---

[66] These are calculated on the following basis:
Good quality architect providing a full build supervision: 8.5% of Project cost + VAT
Undercover construction: R16K per M²
Pergolas construction: R3.7K per M²

No allowance has been made for escalation or contingency.

18.4 Property Marketing and Purchase Costs

The costs of both marketing and purchasing property in South Africa are significant.

Marketing Costs

The vendor is responsible for paying the estate agent's commission, which usually ranges up to 7.5%. There is no regulation in South Africa as to the commission rate that should be charged. You may frequently find that the same property is marketed by multiple estate agents, with the successful agent taking all the commission. The vendor often insists on marketing the property at the price that they choose, which may be significantly higher than the agent's valuation.

Purchasing Costs

If the property is being purchased directly from a developer, then VAT at 14% is applicable. Generally, this is included in the asking price, but check. If the property is a resale and not being bought from a company, then VAT isn't applicable but transfer duty and conveyancing fees are.

18 BUYING PROPERTY

The transfer fee is a once off fee payable prior to the transfer of the property. It is collected by the transferring attorneys on behalf of the South African Revenue Service (SARS). Transfer fees as of 1st March 2017 are:

- There is no Transfer Duty on property under R900,000
- From R900K to R1.25M, transfer duty is calculated at 3% of the value above R900K. (You don't pay transfer duty on the first R900K)
- From R1.25M to R1.75M, transfer duty is calculated at 6% on the value above R1.25M plus a flat rate of R10,500.
- From R1.75M to R2.25M, transfer duty is calculated at 8% on the value above R1.75M plus a flat rate of R40,500.
- From R2.25M to R10M, transfer duty is calculated at 11% of the value above R2.25M plus R80,500.
- From R10M and above, transfer duty is calculated at 13% of the value exceeding R10M Plus R933,000.

Conveyancing fees are for the services the transferring attorneys provide to get your property transferred from its previous owner to you, and to get the property registered in your name. This fee is payable to the attorneys prior to transfer. The fee is based on tariffs recommended by the Law Society[67], however, they are negotiable. Some examples are:

- From R1M to R5M, conveyance costs are R17,200 for the first R1M plus R700 per R100K or part thereof.
- Over R5M, conveyance costs are R45,200 for the first R5M plus R350 per R100K or part thereof above that.

Since property transactions are expensive, you need to ensure that the property will meet both your immediate and longer term needs as you progress into your more senior years.

---

[67] Law Society, see www.lssa.org.za

18.5 Other Considerations

When viewing property, the following points may be worthy of consideration:

- Property orientation with respect to both sunlight for the swimming pool and wind direction if in the Western Cape.
- Thatched roofs may be very attractive but they will adversely impact on the annual running costs of the property. You should anticipate a substantial increase in your house insurance premiums, circa five times, due to the increased fire risk, together with the need to maintain (comb) them every five years. For these reasons, you may struggle when you to come to resell the property.
- Many properties may have electrical underfloor heating. South Africa used to have one of the lowest electrical tariffs in the world. However, today it is now on a par with the UK, and Eskom has requested a further 19.9% increase for 2018. Thus, such heating is likely to be too expensive to operate.
- If you are considering buying a property within an estate, review the current levies, and more importantly, how they have changed over the last few years.
- Be suspicious of large rugs covering beautifully tiled floors. Sometimes they are used to cover up extensive cracking. Similarly, investigate any discolouration on the tiled roof surface. In one particular case, the roof had taken on some beautiful rustic colours, only to reveal on further examination that the wrong fastenings had been used to attach the tile, and they were simply rusting away.

18.6 The Purchasing Process

Don't be put off by a high asking price, as most sellers are willing to negotiate. This is particularly true for the higher end property. Vendors generally presume that buyers will bargain and rarely expect to receive the asking price. However, some vendors can have unrealistic expectations, circa R2M over the market value, and even though the property may have been on the market for a year, they simply won't budge on price. You can always start at 10% less, as the vendor can always put a counter-proposal.

Voetstoots

The vendor, under South African law, is automatically held liable for latent defects, whether or not he knew of them at the time of the sale. To avoid this common law liability, a Voetstoots (buy as seen) clause is included in a sale agreement to protect the vendor from any action which the purchaser may initiate, should any latent defect be discovered. However, this protection is imperfect.

Voetstoots protects the vendor from any claims arising from patent defects. Patent defects are flaws that would be clearly visible during a normal inspection of the property. Latent defects refer to faults that are not immediately obvious and are hidden from view. Examples could include faulty pool pumps and geysers or defects that have been concealed behind a cabinet. The vendor is only excused from liability for latent defects where he himself was unaware of the problem at the time of the sale. If a vendor knowingly conceals a latent defect, he will be liable to the purchaser for the cost of its repair.

Thus, the purchaser should ensure he is aware of all patent defects and any latent defects that have been disclosed prior to making an offer on a property. If you lack the necessary knowledge to carry out a comprehensive home inspection, please consider using a professional service. One example is

House Check[68]. For a very modest fee, in comparison to the cost of the property, they will provide a comprehensive report and include estimates for any remedial work. This can always be used as part of the negotiation process.

Letter of Offer
Offers to buy a property are made in writing, but should be made with extreme care, as they become binding if accepted by the vendor. However, within the letter of offer, it is possible to insert conditions such as:

- Selling an existing property.
- Satisfactory home inspection etc.

However, excessive conditions may make the offer less attractive. There are only four scenarios under which an offer to purchase will lapse if it has not been accepted by the vendor.

- Lapse after the specified time period. The offer should specify a validity period. If one is not specified, then it will lapse after a reasonable time. This leads to ambiguity, so it is best eliminated by specifying a date.
- Offer is revoked. The offer may be revoked by the purchaser, providing the seller hasn't accepted it and the offer is not identified as being irrevocable.
- Vendor rejects the offer. The offer ceases to exist as soon as the vendor rejects it. However, the vendor may cross out the original amount that the purchaser has offered, write in a higher amount and initialise the change. This is considered to be a counter-offer. Nevertheless, the original offer has lapsed.

---

[68] House Check, see www.housecheck.co.za

- Death of either party. If the buyer or vendor dies before the offer has been accepted, it will automatically lapse. However, in the instance where the offer has been signed and accepted, all rights and duties arising from the contract will be passed to the deceased estate.

The one exception to the above is where the property is priced at less than R250K. Under such circumstances, you are allowed a 5 day cooling off period during which the buyer can cancel the offer, provided he does so in writing.

Conveyancing Attorney
Once the vendor has accepted the letter of offer, he will appoint a conveyancing attorney. The purchaser will then be required to pay a deposit, typically 10%. The deposit will be invested on your behalf and any interest earned will ultimately be credited to your account. The attorney will request a variety of documents from you to ensure compliance with the FICA (Financial Intelligence Act) and other requirements. Documentation will include:

- Certified passport picture page.
- Proof of address (rental agreement).
- Bank details (bank statements stamped by the bank).
- Data sheet for SARS (South African Revenue Service).
- Various Affidavits.

Thereafter, the only remaining action is to transfer the balance of the funds when requested by the attorney, which is typically 8 to 12 weeks after the initial offer.

19. Wills

This section has been written after careful research. However, that is not a substitute for advice from a professional who can consider your personal circumstances.

19.1 Immovable vs. Movable Objects

Once you retire it is likely that you will start transferring assets to South Africa, and at that point, you should consider whether a South African Will is required. The key questions that you need to answer are:

- Am I going to purchase land/property e.g. immovable property?
- Where am I going to be domiciled?

In common law jurisdictions, a distinction is made between movable property, such as goods and immovable property, such as a house or land. For movable property, the relevant law is where you are domiciled, whereas for immovable objects, it is where they are physically located. Hence, if you are visiting South Africa on a temporary visa and acquired a property, then it could be argued that you are still domiciled in the UK. Thus, you may wish to consider two Wills. Your UK Will covers your movable objects such as your investments whilst a South African Will would be required to cover your immovable property.

One word of caution concerning two Wills is that you must be careful about revoking previous Wills. In England and Wales, Wills commonly include a clause revoking all previous Wills. Thus, if your English Will contains such a clause it is likely to have the effect of revoking your South African Will.

19.2 Definition of Domicile

Domicile of Origin
Your domicile is the country where you have your permanent home or with which you have a substantial connection. When you're born, you're automatically assigned to the same domicile as your parents, which is defined as your domicile of origin.

Deemed Domicile
For UK citizens living abroad, there is also a concept of 'deemed domicile', which is important when calculating inheritance tax on your estate when you die. 'Deemed domicile' means that even if you are not domiciled in the UK, under general law HMRC could treat you as domiciled in the UK at the time of a transfer if you were:

- Domiciled in the UK within the three years immediately before the transfer, or
- Resident in the UK in at least 17 of the 20 income tax years of assessment ending with the year in which you make a transfer.

Domicile of Choice
The minimum requirements for changing your domicile, assuming you are older than sixteen are:

- Relocating from one country to another.
- Providing strong evidence that you intend to live in the new country permanently e.g. buy a home in South Africa and apply for permanent residency.

Hence, if you consider yourself to be domiciled in South Africa, then one Will may suffice if you only have very simple assets e.g. a single bank account in the UK. However, if you have more complex assets, or a significant balance in your UK bank account, then two separate Wills would be recommended, with separate executors.

19.3 Dying in South Africa without a Will

If you die without a Will, it means you have died 'intestate.' When this happens, the intestacy laws of South Africa, assuming you are domiciled here, will determine how your property is distributed upon your death. An abbreviated set of rules are:

- Spouse with no descendants -> All left to the spouse
- Descendants with no spouse -> All left to the descendent
- Spouse with descendants -> The total estate is divided by the number parties, to give a share. The spouse receives the greater of the R250,000 or a share. The residue is divided up equally amongst the remaining descendants.

19.4 Will Services

Many banks will offer free or at nominal costs Will writing services, assuming they are nominated as executor, together with a Will custody service. For example, FNB (First National Bank) will email you a Will template, which you can complete. This will then allow them to create the required Will, for free, for you to review. The only costs are for storage, as detailed below:

- Annual custody - Annual fee R100 (£5.95)
- Custody for life - R500 (£29.76)

All of the above options include all future Will reviews at no additional cost. Safekeeping of the Will is essential, as the High Court requires that on death the original Will is lodged when reporting the estate, as copies are not acceptable.

19 WILLS

The cost of execution services on behalf of a deceased estate is governed by the tariffs laid down by law in terms of the Administration of Estate's Act. The executor's fees are up to 3.99% of the total value of the assets dealt with in the estate and not just the value of the assets left by the deceased. This excludes proceeds of policies payable outside the estate, which are included only for estate duty purposes.

Such costs would normally apply on the death of the first spouse, and not just on the death of the surviving spouse. For larger estates, and also on the death of the first spouse, such fees appear to be excessive. It is possible, with some executors, to negotiate fees upfront and have it written into the Will.

Executors' services are expensive, which in turn may cause liquidity problems with the estate. This can force the surviving spouse to sell assets just to meet the executor's fees. One solution is to take out a life policy just to cover such fees. Alternatively, can the surviving spouse execute the Will, and purchase any professional services that may be required on an ad hoc basis?

19.5 Joint Wills

It is possible you may be offered a joint Will. This is really a single Will signed by two people, usually a married couple, leaving all their assets to each other. On the face of it, this is a simple and sensible approach. Typically, a joint Will will state that:

- When one spouse dies, the survivor will inherit everything, and
- When the second spouse dies, everything will go to the children.

A joint Will may contain a provision that neither spouse can change or revoke the Will alone. Thus, on the death of the first spouse, the Will becomes irrevocable, and that is the problem. Circumstances change and the survivor may wish to give an adult child some of his inheritance early as perhaps a down payment. However, a joint Will would prevent this, so check first. This lack of flexibility means that joint Wills may not be the best choice.

20. Miscellaneous

20.1 South African Post Office (SAPO)

Unfortunately, I have to say that this is probably not the best postal service in the world, particularly for incoming mail. In fairness, the staff are always helpful and we have never knowingly lost mail.

A simple single page letter to the UK takes about 5 working days. A larger A4 sized envelope containing 6 sheets was sent to Trinidad and it took eight weeks. Mail from the UK typically takes 10 days and a small parcel from the UK took 7 weeks. Using a courier service from the UK doesn't automatically guarantee a quick delivery. In our case, we used a courier service, LandMark, selected off the Parcel2Go[69] website, which offered a super economy service for 4+ days at a cost of £20, compared with TNT Express offering a 3 day service for £10 more. In hindsight, this was false economy, as 4+ days ended up being 7 weeks, and the tracking information, once it got to South Africa, was non-existent, beyond the fact that it had arrived somewhere in the country. In this particular case, although the package was couriered out to South Africa, it was then simply injected into the ordinary mail system. So, if you select a courier service, ensure that they provide an end to end service, rather than just a hybrid service using SAPO as the delivery agent.

In conclusion, it is difficult to recommend SAPO for any critical or time sensitive mail.

---

[69] Parcel2Go, see www.parcel2go.com

20.2 Bank Charges

In may come as a surprise to UK residents that in South Africa you pay for banking services. Specifically, you are likely to pay separately for:

- Transactional (cheque) account.
- Investment/saving account.
- Credit card.

Your transactional account fee will typically include a list of pre-packaged services, with other services attracting additional costs. As an example, an account may permit so many cash withdrawals from the bank's ATM machine. Withdrawals in excess of the permitted number are charged at 1.85%, not entirely insignificant. Generally, you can minimise some of these costs by maintaining a qualifying balance. As an example, your transactional account may qualify for a rebate of its monthly fees if you maintain a qualifying balance either in that account or in a linked investment/saving account. However, because of the cost of handling cash, banks are actively trying to migrate their customers to plastic or Electronic Funds Transfer (EFT) using an appropriate App on their mobile phone.

Most of the banks offer some form of customer reward program. Some of these, for example, eBucks can be beneficial by offering discounted travel.[70]

---

[70] eBucks, see www.ebucks.com/web/eBucks

20.3 Local Credit Cards

Getting a local credit card can be a bit of a challenge. This is because as part of the application process you will be subject to credit scoring and unfortunately it appears that the checks are against your South African ID number. Not having one, results in automatic rejection. One of the downsides of emigrating is that you lose your credit history and effectively you are starting again from scratch. It is perhaps made more difficult, as you are now retired and no longer have a company salary. So, when you apply for a credit card, you will need to provide proof of income. This could be in the form of a statement from your pension administrator or perhaps just bank statements. In our case, we had to find an understanding banker who made a manual application on our behalf. Even then it took six weeks before a decision was made.

20.4 Driving Licences

Temporary Resident
All drivers must have a valid driving licence from their country of residence. You can drive in South Africa on a British licence or any other licence that is printed in English. However, if the licence is not printed in English, then you will need to obtain an International Drivers Permit.

Permanent Resident

Once permanent residency has been obtained, holders of a foreign licence (or IDP) have one year in which to convert their foreign driving licence to a South African one, after which, failure to convert will render the licence invalid both to convert or to drive with. The conversion process, assuming your existing licence is in English, requires the following:

- Identification document and a certified copy.
- Four passport photographs.
- Current foreign driving licence.
- Proof of permanent residency in South Africa.
- Proof that he/she was not permanently or ordinarily resident in the RSA at the time the foreign licence or permit was originally issued (for example a passport, permanent residence permit or visa).
- Confirmation from a Driving Licence Issuing Authority that the person is in possession of a valid driving licence. For a UK licence, you will have to contact the DVLA.[71]
- In the case of an IDP (International Drivers permit), the driving licence on the authority of which such permit was issued.
- Proof of address.

If you do not have permanent residency, you cannot get a South African driving licence.

---

[71] DVLA, see www.gov.uk/browse/driving/driving-licences

20.5 Post Office Box

Generally, in the UK your residential address is also used as your postal address. This isn't always true in South Africa, where our rented house didn't have a letterbox or post box. In the case of mail delivered to our residential address, it is just pushed under the garage door. When you fill in any application forms, you will often have the option to enter both a physical address and a postal address. In our case, we anticipated renting accommodation in different locations but decided we wanted a single postal address for all our mail. Hence, a post box was required. This can be obtained either from the South African Post Office (SAPO) or from certain private companies such as PostNet[72]. The annual cost of a SAPO box is R410 (£24.40) or for pensioners, there is a reduced rate of R256 (£15.24). If it is a separate physical box that you have access to from outside the Post Office building, rather than just an internal box (virtual box) within the building, then there is a key deposit of R30 (£1.79).

20.6 TV Licence

Many people find it frustrating to pay for a TV licence, even though they will never use the device to receive a TV broadcast signal. In terms of the Broadcasting Act, No 4 of 1999, any person or entity that has in its possession and/or uses a TV set must have a TV licence. Thus, retailers take the view that customers must either purchase or produce a valid TV licence when buying any television.

Licences can be obtained from SABC (South African Broadcasting Corporation) licensing department. There are six different types of licence available but you will need the 'Domestic Licence'. This covers all TVs at your residential address at an annual cost of R265 (£15.77).[73]

---

[72] PostNet, see www.postnet.co.za
[73] SABC licensing department, see www.tvlic.co.za/tvlic

20.7 Informing the UK Government on Arrival

If you leave the UK on a permanent basis, then you should inform HMRC (Her Majesty's Revenue and Customs) to ensure you get taxed on the correct basis. You should do this by completing form P85 and return it to HMRC, together with parts 2 and 3 of your P45.[74]

---

[74] HMRC P85, see www.gov.uk/tax-right-retire-abroad-return-to-uk

Appendices

Appendix 1: Useful Links

1.1 Foreign Exchange Currency Brokers
1. World First (http://www.worldfirst.com) [75]
2. Smart Currency Exchange (http://www.smartcurrencyexchange.com)
3. TorFX (http://www.torfx.com)
4. Moneycorp (http://www.moneycorp.com)
5. Interactive Brokers (http://www.interactivebrokers.com)[76]

1.2 Immigration Agents
1. Intergate Immigration (http://www.intergate-immigration.com) [77]
2. Imcosa (http://www.imcosa.co.za)
3. New World Immigration (http://www.nwivisas.com)

---

[75] World First - Extensively used and recommended prior to departure. However, their licensing prevents them from servicing clients once they have permanently relocated to South Africa so an alternative solution will be required.

[76] Interactive Brokers - Very competitive for spot and limit orders; generally aimed at professional or more frequent traders. Less suitable for forward contracts.

[77] Integrate Immigration - Very professional and helpful. Assisted with our temporary retirement visas. Recommended.

APPENDIX 1: USEFUL LINKS

1.3 South African Banks
1. Capitec (http://www.capitecbank.co.za)
2. FNB (http://www.fnb.co.za)[78]
3. Nedbank (http://www.nedbank.co.za)[79]
4. Absa (http://www.absa.co.za)
5. Standard Bank (http://www.standardbank.co.za)

1.4 Mobile Phone Networks
1. Vodacom (http://www.vodacom.co.za)
2. Telkom Mobile (http://www.telkom.co.za)
3. MTN (http://www.mtn.co.za)
4. Cell C (http://www.cellc.co.za)

1.5 Medical Aid Schemes
1. Discovery (http://www.discovery.co.za)[80]
2. TopMed Mobile (http://www.topmed.co.za)
3. BestMed (http://www.bestmed.co.za)
4. Medimed (http://www.medimed.co.za)
5. Bonitas (http://www.bonitas.co.za)
6. Momentum (http://www.momentum.co.za)
7. Fedhealth (http://www.fedhealth.co.za)
8. Genesis (http://www.genesismedical.co.za)

---

[78] FNB (First National Bank) - Recommended. Good online banking and mobile apps with extensive branch and customer support.

[79] Nedbank - You are assigned a relationship manager with all matters being routed through this contact. Thus, branch can provide only very limited support. This didn't really work for us.

[80] Discovery - The largest Medical Aid scheme provider in South Africa with an extensive variety of plans with good cover for chronic conditions. A safe choice.

1.6 Medical Aid Gap Insurance
1. Total Risk Administrators (http://www.totalrisksa.co.za)
2. Zestlife (http://www.zestlife.co.za)
3. Sanlam (http://www.sanlam.co.za)
4. Stratum Benefits (http://www.stratumbenefits.co.za)
5. Liberty (http://www.liberty.co.za)
6. Cura Administrators (http://www.curaadmin.co.za)

1.7 Dental Insurance
1. Drum Company (http://www.drum.company)[81]
2. 2. Affinity Dental (http://www.affinitydental.co.za)

1.8 Medical Aid Brokers
1. Independent Medical Aid Specialists (http://www.medicalaidcomparisons.co.za)
2. CureMed (http://www.curemed.co.za)
3. IFC (http://www.medicalaid-quotes.co.za)
4. Medcon (http://www.medcon.co.za)
5. Peter Pyburn (http://www.peterpyburn.co.za)[82]

1.9 Car Insurance Underwriters
1. King Price (http://www.kingprice.co.za)
2. OUTSurance (http://www.outsurance.co.za)
3. Auto General (http://www.autogen.co.za)
4. Discovery (http://www.discovery.co.za/car-and-home-insurance)

---

[81] Drum Company - They offer a range of policies that cover both basic and advanced dentistry together with an extensive network of providers. If you decide that you want dental insurance, rather than just 'pay as you go', then they are recommended.

[82] Peter Pyburn - One of the smaller and more responsive brokers offering a personalised service.

APPENDIX 1: USEFUL LINKS

1.10 Real Estate Agents/Web Sites
1. Property24 (http://www.property24.com)
2. PrivateProperty (http://www.privateproperty.co.za)
3. Lew Geffen Sotheby's (https://www.sothebysrealty.co.za/)
4. Harcourts (https://harcourts.co.za)
5. Seeff (https://www.seeff.com/)
6. Pam Golding (http://www.pamgolding.co.za)
7. Engel & Volkers (https://www.engelvoelkers.com/en-za/south-africa)
8. Fine and Country (http://www.fineandcountry.com/sa)

Appendix 2: Chronic Medical Conditions

All medical aid schemes, but not necessarily health insurers, must cover for the diagnosis, treatment and care of the following 27 chronic conditions:

1. Addison's disease
2. Asthma
3. Bipolar mood disorder
4. Bronchiectasis
5. Cardiac failure
6. Cardiomyopathy
7. Chronic obstructive pulmonary disorder
8. Chronic renal disease
9. Coronary artery disease
10. Crohn's disease
11. Diabetes insipidus
12. Diabetes Type 1
13. Diabetes Type 2
14. Dysrhythmias
15. Epilepsy
16. Glaucoma
17. Haemophilia
18. HIV/AIDS
19. Hyperlipidaemia
20. Hypertension
21. Hypothyroidism
22. Multiple sclerosis
23. Parkinson's disease
24. Rheumatoid arthritis
25. Schizophrenia
26. Systemic lupus erythematosus
27. Ulcerative colitis

APPENDIX 2: CHRONIC MEDICAL CONDITIONS

Medical aid plans may cover additional conditions but the above reflects the minimum number of chronic conditions that must be covered. Once your chronic condition has been diagnosed, a care plan would be issued by your medical aid scheme which, for example, will detail the standard of care that they will fund. For example, this may include, on an annual basis, a number of family/specialist consultations, together with on-going monitoring tests.

Appendix 3: Medical Aid Terminology

3.1 Waiting Period
There are two types of waiting period that can be imposed by the underwriters of the medical aid schemes.

General Waiting Period
New members to a medical aid scheme will automatically have an exclusion of 3 months.

Pre-existing Conditions
These may be subject to a further exclusion period but this cannot exceed 12 months from the start of the scheme.

However, in either case you are covered for medical emergencies from the date you join the scheme.

3.2 Prescribed Minimum Benefits (PMB)
They are a set of minimum benefits that medical schemes must give to all their members – according to the law [Medical Schemes Act of 1998 (Act number 131 of 1998)]. The cover it gives includes the diagnosis, treatment and cost of ongoing care for:

- Any life-threatening emergency medical condition.
- A defined set of 270 diagnoses.
- 27 chronic conditions - see appendix 2 for further detail.

APPENDIX 3: MEDICAL AID TERMINOLOGY

All medical schemes in South Africa have to include the Prescribed Minimum Benefits in the benefit options they offer to their members. However, hospital cash back schemes and health insurance costs are not covered by the act. Medical aid schemes will have a list of conditions that are not covered, e.g. cosmetic surgery. Such exclusions don't apply to PMB. For example, if you develop septicaemia after cosmetic surgery, then the septicaemia will be covered by the PMB, since they are concerned with diagnosis and treatment and not how you developed the condition.

The requirements to access PMBs are:

- The condition must be on the list of defined PMB conditions.
- The treatment needed must match the treatments in the defined benefits on the PMB list.
- You must use the Scheme's designated service providers.

PMBs will not be available if you have just joined a medical aid scheme for the first time and you are still within a waiting period.

3.3 Late Joiners

Medical aid costs on a member basis are not age related. As such, they aren't loaded with an age premium. However, the costs will increase with inflation. When a member is young and healthy he is likely to make few claims on the scheme compared to an older member who has greater needs. Nevertheless, they would both pay the same premium. Thus, there is a possibility that younger members may delay joining a scheme until later in life. To protect the scheme financially there is the concept of a late joiner penalty. The penalty depends on the applicant's age and number of previous years he has been in any previous medical aid scheme. Membership of private medical schemes which are not medical aid e.g. BUPA and Cigna do not count.

There is no late joiner penalty for applicants who are aged 35 or younger.

The calculation of the late joiner penalty is as follows:

Gap = Age - 35 - Number of previous years of medical aid.

Suppose the applicant is aged 59 with no previous medical aid then the gap would become (59-35) 24 years.

Based on the gap the percentage penalty is calculated as follows:

- 0 - 4 years: 5% of the contribution.
- 5- 14 years: 25% of the contribution.
- 15-24 years: 50% of the contribution.
- 25+ years: 75% contribution.

So, in the above case, the applicant with a gap of 24 years would be subject to a 50% increase in contribution. Where this gets a little bit more complicated is that the penalty is applied only to the risk based element, as opposed to the day to day element, of the premium.

3.4 Medical Scheme Tariff

A medical scheme will have a tariff, which is the maximum it will pay for a consultation or procedure. If the procedures or consultation costs more than the agreed tariff, then the member is responsible for the difference. However, please see Gap Cover and Designated Service Provider (DSP).

APPENDIX 3: MEDICAL AID TERMINOLOGY

3.5 Designated Service Provider

A scheme may have an arrangement with designated providers such as doctors, hospitals and pharmacists such that they will provide the required services at the medical scheme tariff. As such, the member should be fully reimbursed for the services provided. The member may choose an alternative provider but he may experience a shortfall between the tariff charged by his selected provider and the medical scheme tariff.

3.6 Gap Cover

This is a short term insurance product and is not part of medical aid but complements such a policy. It can only be used in conjunction with medical aid. There are two major gaps in medical aid which such a policy addresses:

Co-Payments
This can arise because the:

- Member voluntarily selects to use a non-designated service provider and thus is responsible for a co-payment.
- Medical aid imposes a sub-limit on certain procedures; you can think of this as an excess on your house insurance. For example, your doctor believes you are suffering from ulcers and requires an upper GI endoscopic examination to confirm the diagnosis. Such a procedure would be covered by your medical aid but subject to a co-payment of R3700.

Fees in-excess of the Scheme Tariff

If the medical practitioner charges at a rate that exceeds the medical scheme tariff, then the excess is the responsibility of the member. For example, the professional fees for a Coronary Bypass could be R40,700 and yet the medical aid pay out could be restricted to R13,700 and thus the member would be responsible for the difference.

Typically, such policies will not cover:

- Upgrades to a private room.
- Pre-admission consultations costs.
- Medication.
- External appliances such as wheelchairs or crutches.
- Home or private nursing.
- Cosmetic procedures.

3.7 Hospital Plan

This category of medical aid covers only hospitalisation together with prescribed minimum benefits.

3.8 Day to Day Benefits

These are out of hospital benefits which may cover fees associated with visits to general/family practitioners, including prescribed medication, dentists and opticians. Such benefits would not be available with a hospital plan.

3.9 Medical Savings Account

More comprehensive plans offer both hospital and day to day benefits. In order to fund the day to day benefits, a proportion of the contribution, typically 15% to 25%, is diverted into a personal saving account. The funds within this account are then used to fund the day to day benefits. If funds remain in the account at the end of the year, then it is simply rolled forward into next year's account. Should the member leave the scheme, then the balance will be paid out.

APPENDIX 3: MEDICAL AID TERMINOLOGY

3.10 Threshold Benefits

The more comprehensive medical aids offer threshold benefits which are designed to cover day to day benefits. Initially, day to day benefits are paid from the medical savings account. Once this is exhausted the member will be required to pay any additional costs up to the self payment gap. Once the self payment gap has been breached, any additional costs will be paid by the scheme. For example, for a single adult member, the following annual limits may apply:

Savings account: R5,004

Self payment gap: R6,196

Threshold level: R11,200

Thus, for day to day expenses, the first R5,004 will be covered directly from the members medical saving account. Once the account is exhausted the next R6,196 will be paid by the member. Should this threshold limit be reached then any further costs will be met by the scheme subject to any sub limits.

Appendix 4: Day to Day Health Care Costs

4.1 Health Care Professional Fees

Ref	Description	Cost
1.	Family Practitioner consultation. This excludes any specialised diagnostic test.	R337 (£20.06)
2.	Opticians - Eye Examination	R200 (£11.90)
3.	Dental inspection + 2 X-rays	R380 (£22.62)

4.2 Diagnostic Tests and Lab Costs

Ref	Description	Cost
1.	Exercise ECG	R540 (£32.13)
2.	Full Cholesterol (Total/LDL/HDL)	R263 (£15.61)
3.	Triglyceride	R109 (£6.50)
4.	Full Blood Count	R136 (£8.10)
5.	Chest X-ray and associated report	R580 (34.52)

APPENDIX 4: DAY TO DAY HEALTH CARE COSTS

4.3 Pharmacist Activities

Ref	Description	Cost
1.	Blood Pressure	R20 (£1.19)
2.	Blood Glucose	R55 (£3.27)
3.	Cholesterol and Lipogram	R90 (£5.36), R175 (£10.42)
4.	HIV Counselling and Testing	R150 (£8.93)
5.	Haemoglobin	R85 (£5.06)
6.	Comprehensive Wellness • Blood pressure/glucose • BMI/Cholesterol	R160 (£9.52)
7.	Basic Wellness • Blood pressure/BMI	R85 (£5.06)
8.	Foot Screenings	R50 (£2.98)
9.	PSA Screenings	R100 (£5.95)
10.	Adult Vaccinations Excludes cost of vaccine	R50 (£2.98)
11.	Diabetes Screening (HbA1C)	R175 (£10.42)

Final Thoughts

A big thank you for reading this book. We hope that you have found it both interesting and informative. If you enjoyed this book, please consider leaving a brief, honest review on Amazon. Reviews help young (at heart) indie authors like myself get noticed.

We fully appreciate that retiring, and particularly retiring abroad, is a major decision. For those of you that have outstanding questions, suggestions for improvements, or would just like to know a little more, then please feel free to reach out to us via email to

RetiringToSouthAfrica@karibi.co.uk.

My wife and I made our decision in 2016 and have no regrets.

Chris Wilson
Pearl Valley, Paarl, Western Cape, South Africa

Printed in Poland
by Amazon Fulfillment
Poland Sp. z o.o., Wrocław